ARAB
KEY WORDS

is a learning aid for those living in Arab countries, visiting the Arab World, doing business with the nations of the Middle East from Morocco to Jordan and the Arabian Peninsula, or for those interested in acquiring the elements of a Semitic language.

The Arabic script has been transliterated throughout to aid quick assimilation, and the commonest two thousand key words in Arabic, with their meanings in English, have been arranged in decreasing order of frequency, with a separate list of numerals and days of the week.

The list is divided into a hundred units of twenty key words each, from which many more words can be derived. For singular nouns, plurals are given if irregular. For masculine adjectives, feminine endings are given if irregular.

David Quitregard, who has been involved with the Arab World and the Arabic language for more than thirty years, has always believed that learners of Arabic are discouraged by the complexities of the Arabic script, and should be able to master all the basic vocabulary for speaking the modern language within the first year of study. Now, with *Arabic Key Words*, the prospective pupil is rewarded for graded efforts by learning the most frequent words first, and leaving rarer words till much later. An Arabic index allows the user to trace each word in the lists, and an English index acts as a cross-checking dictionary. For the first time it is possible to learn Arabic vocabulary in an orderly manner.

ARABIC
KEY WORDS

the basic 2,000-word vocabulary
arranged by frequency in a
hundred units

with comprehensive English and
transliterated Arabic indexes

DAVID QUITREGARD

The Oleander Press

The Oleander Press
17 Stansgate Avenue
Cambridge CB2 2QZ
England

The Oleander Press
80 Eighth Avenue, Suite 303
New York
N.Y. 10011
U.S.A.

British Library Cataloguing in Publication Data

Quitregard, David
  Arabic key words. (Oleander language and
literature; v. 16)
  1. Arabic language–Dictionaries–English
  2. English language–Dictionaries–Arabic
  I. Title   II. Series
  492

  ISBN 0-906672-27-9

Printed in Great Britain by Bell and Bain Ltd, Glasgow

CONTENTS

Introduction

Arabic Key Words has been designed as an efficient, logical and practical computer-based word-list for anglophone learners of Arabic in their first year and second year. It has also proved valuable as a revision tool for more advanced students.

The basic two thousand 'key' words are so called because by learning these one unlocks the door to many thousand more words: plurals from singulars, feminines from masculines, parts of the imperfect from the infinite form (that is, in practice, the third person singular of the imperfect). Regular forms of the present and perfect are set out before Unit 1.

One purpose of this technique is to stimulate confidence in the learning of Arabic by teaching the commonest words first, and leaving the less common till later. Nothing is more daunting to the beginner than encountering dozens of rare words which have to be learnt to make sense of a passage, yet may not recur in reading over a period of several years.

A simplified form of transliteration has been used for the beginner, who will quickly recognise from the sound that the apostrophe has been used for both *'ain* and hamza, 's' for *sīn* and *sād*, 't' for both *tā'*; letters, 'h' for both *hā'* letters, 'd' for three 'd' letters in addition to the obvious 'th' for *thā'*, 'j' for *jīm*, 'kh' for *khā'*, 'dh' for *dhāl*, 'r' for *rā'*, 'sh' for *shīn*, 'gh' for *ghain*, 'f' for *fā'*, 'q' for *qāf*, 'k' for *kāf*, 'l' for *lām*, 'm' for *mīm*, 'n' for *nūn*, 'a' for *'alif*, 'w' for *waw*, and 'y' for *yā*. The three vowels when short are shown a, i, and u, and when long ā, ī, and ū. This does not of course represent the pronunciation throughout the Arab World. It is suggested that learners acquaint themselves with the Arabic script as soon as possible, but as *Arabic Key Words* was compiled with busy professional people in mind, the time for this study may not be available even if the motivation exists.

Arabic Key Words is intended to be used with a modern conventional grammar and a conventional dictionary, such as the latest edition of Hans Wehr's *A Dictionary of Modern Written Arabic*, but a massive dictionary has been found in practice to unnerve a beginner, while most available readers introduce too early many words which may be arbitrary, recondite or advanced. At this sensitive phase, when interest in learning Arabic can be so easily encouraged or discouraged, it is suggested that the student should learn units of about twenty 'key' words each day, thus mastering two thousand such words by the end of the first year. Only then will she or he be ready to accumulate some arbitrary words of low occurrence, many of which will in any case be related by their root to words already learnt. Computer-based methods are by now fully familiar in mathematics and the sciences, but statistical sampling has hitherto been rarely practised in language-learning, probably because of the difficulty of establishing a sufficiently large and accurate up-to-date sample to make the frequency list reliable. The Oleander Press pioneered this approach in *French Key Words* (1984) by Xavier-Yves Escande, *Italian Key Words* (1992) by Gianpaolo Intronati, *Spanish Key Words* (1993) by Pedro Casal, and they announce *German Key Words* (1994) by Dieter Zahn.

The Units

Each of the hundred units is self-contained, Unit 1 including the twenty commonest words, Unit 2 the next commonest and so on. The key word is followed by its plural if an irregular noun. A verb is shown by its third personal singular imperfect form, which is always translated beginning with 'to'. *Masculine nouns and adjectives* form their feminine by adding *a*, if regular. So *maftūh* (open) becomes *maftūha* in the feminine. Masculine nouns form their plurals by adding *ūna* if regular (or 'sound' as we say in Arabic), so *khayyāt* (tailor) becomes *khayyātūna*, and *hasan* (good) becomes *hasanūna*. Dictionaries do not give the sound masculine plural, which applies also to verbal participles. The dual number is formed by adding the suffix *ani* in the nominative and *ayni* in the oblique, so *malik* (king) becomes *malikāni* and *malikayni* and *malika* (queen) becomes *malikatāni* and *malikatayni*. *Feminine nouns and adjectives* form their plural by lengthening the last *ā* and adding *t* if regular. So *sifāra* (embassy) becomes *sifārāt*, and *kathīra* (many, much) becomes *kathīrāt*. The regular (sound) feminine plural is of course not confined to female beings, but is used with many abstract nouns, infinitives, and other feminine forms. Adjectives agree with their nouns in gender, number and case, except for broken plurals and for sound feminine plurals which have adjectives in the feminine singular, as a rule.

Regular verbs are represented by the triliteral root *k-t-b*, to

Regular verbs are represented by the triliteral root *k-t-b*, to write, conjugated in the present and imperfect tenses in a separate table just before the hundred units. Though verbs appear only in their perfect tense, third person singular masculine, their positions within the hundred units has been determined from the total occurrence of all their parts.

Many Arabic words may be translated by a number of English equivalents. It would be counter-productive, in a work designed to stimulate interest in a fascinating language rather than to clog the memory, to list all such equivalents, so only the statistically most common have been cited, with the commonest of all first. When consulting the two indexes, therefore, the reader who cannot find a given word should try to think of synonyms or near-synonyms if a certain word seems to be omitted.

Apart from the numeral one, the units omit all numerals, which are listed (1-21, 100, 1,000) before the hundred units begin.

The Indexes

The two indexes permit the reader to use *Arabic Key Words* as a basic transliterated dictionary, but let it be repeated that the best available dictionary should be purchased to use in conjunction with the present aid, if it is intended to continue with Arabic past the elementary stage. The best possible grammar should be purchased too, reflecting standard classical Arabic or the colloquial language of the area where the reader lives.

The first fourteen words are so common that they account for 38.72% of total occurrences in a lexical universe of nearly two million words; the first hundred account for 63.85% of total occurrences; and the first thousand for 84.19%. This means in practical terms that anyone who masters the vocabulary in *Arabic Key Words* will need only another 15% or so to cover the entire vocabulary encountered in newspapers, magazines, books, radio and television.

The Sources

The word-list has been based on a collaborative computer-based project devised by the author. Some two million words were sampled using all types of publication such as fiction, drama, essays, historical, geographical and scientific works, magazines from nine countries, newspapers from fourteen countries, films from seven countries, radio programmes from twelve countries, television programmes from eight countries, children's books and literary histories.

Comparison with word-lists in other languages indicate that with few exceptions the 2,000 commonest words remain constant over a period of several decades, perhaps over centuries, because mankind's main preoccupations remain essentially constant. We have removed words considered offensive, borrowings from foreign languages, and slang or colloquial terminology of purely local or regional interest.

In addition to my long-term debts to colleagues, friends, associates and collaborators in the U.S.A., Europe, and throughout the Arab World, I must place on special record my gratitude to teams at Al-Azhar University, Harvard University, and Oxford University who at one time or another took responsibility for analysing groups of books, journals and newspapers, and in particular to Professor Wolfgang Bartsch, Dr Ibrahim Mansuri, Dr E. Wenner-Gren, Dr Muhammad Salim ad-Dib, Faud and Fawzi al-Khouri formerly in Lebanon, Cynthia Hatzidakis in Yemen, Mabruk Fakhro in Qatar, Abdulhamid bin Sulaiman in Abu Dhabi and Saudi Arabia, Nacer Jalal ed-Dine formerly of al-Qarawiyin University, Fez, Fatma Goujiane in Algiers, Abdullatif Saif in Damascus, and Earl Mantice, Flushing, New York. For double-checking thanks go to Miranda Siddiqi, and for help with typing thanks to Lalia Galcik, Sasha Radmall, and Felicity Purves.

DAVID QUITREGARD

Numerals

1	Wāhad
2	Ithnîn
3	Thalātha
4	Arb'a
5	Khamsa
6	Sitta
7	Sab'a
8	Thamāniya
9	Tis'a
10	'Ashara
11	Ihd'ashar
12	Ithn'ashar
13	Thalāthat'ashar
14	Arb'at'ashar
15	Khamsat'ashar
16	Sitt'ashar
17	Sab'at'ashar
18	Thamant'ashar
19	Tis'at'ashar
20	'Ashrîn
21	Wāhad wa 'ashrin, etc.
100	Mîya
1,000	Alf

Regular Verb in the Present Tense

Most verbs in Arabic have a triliteral root (k-t-b, write; sh-r-b, drink) and form their present and past in the following regular manner:

anā aktubu	I write
anta taktubu	you (*s.masc.*) write
anti taktubĭna	you (*s.fem.*) write
hŭwa yaktubu	he writes
hĭya taktubu	she writes
antumā taktubāni	you (*dual, m.f.*) write
humā yaktubāni	they (*dual, m.f.*) write
nahnu naktubu	we write
antum taktubūna	you (*pl. masc.*) write
antunna taktubna	you (*pl. fem.*) write
hum yaktubūna	they (*masc.*) write
hunna yaktubna	they (*fem.*) write

But when the verb in the third person *precedes* the subject it is always in the singular:

kataba 'l-mu'allimāni	the two teachers wrote
kataba 'l-mu'allimūna	the teachers (three or more) wrote

This tense, both continuous present and habitual present, is often known as the imperfect tense in Arabic, because the action has not been completed.

Regular Verb in the Perfect Tense

Actions that have been completed use the triliteral root in a similarly regular manner:

anā katabtu	I wrote, or have written
anta katabta	you (*s.masc.*) have written
anti katabti	you (*s.fem.*) have written
hŭwa kataba	he has written
hiya katabat	she has written
antumā or antunna katabtumā	you (*dual, m.f.*) have written
humā katabā	they two (*masc.*) have written
humā katabatā	they two (*fem.*) have written
nahnu katabnā	we have written
antum katabtum	you (*pl. masc.*) have written
antunna katabtunna	you (*pl. fem.*) have written
hum katabŭ	they (*masc.*) have written
hunna katabna	they (*fem.*) have written

Unit 1

al-	the
(changing before a 'sun' letter, e.g. ash-shams, the sun)	
min	of, from
kāna	to be (*lit.* he, it was)
wa	and
an	that, to
fa	and
fī	in
lā	no, not
hūwa, hīya	he, she, it (*m.f.*)
aw	or
ilā	to, towards
li	to, for, because of
'alā	on
bi	with, by
anā	I
hādha, hādhihi	this (*m., f.*)
dhālika, tilka	that (*m., f.*)
Allah	God
wāhad, wahda	one (*m., f.*)
ba'd	after

Unit 2

mā	not
na'm	yes
'Arab	Arab
ma'a	with, in spite of
hunā	here
qabla	before
a, hal	? (interrogative particle)
hunāka	there
alāna	now
fawqa	over, above, on
anna	that
jiddan	very
kabîr (*pl.* kibār)	big, large
hamdu	praise
tahta	under, below
kayf?	how
anta	you (*s., masc.*)
wājid	much, very
bas (*in classical Arabic* faqat)	only
sayyāra	car

Unit 3

bayt (*pl.* buyūt)	house
rajul (*pl.* rijāl)	man
thumma	then
yawm	day (al-yawm, today)
bukra (*in classical* Arabic ghadan)	tomorrow
anti	you (*s.fem.*)
dāiman	always
shay' (*pl.* ashyā')	thing
'an	about, from
hum	they (*pl. masc.*)
bayna	between, among
hukūma	government
'inda	at, near
aydan	also
ams	yesterday
kull	all, every
wizāra	ministry
nafs (*pl.* nufus, anfus)	self
khās	special
antum	you (*pl. masc.*)

Unit 4

mā	what
ba'd	some
layla (*pl.* layāl)	night
malik (*pl.* mulūk)	king
kathĭr (*pl.* kithār, kathĭrūn)	many, very
shakhs (*pl.* ashkhās)	someone, person
lākin, walākin	but
faqat	only
mumkin	possible
dākhil	inside
qāla	to say (*lit.* 'he said')
awwal (*f.* ūlā)	first
sā'a	hour, clock
jadĭd (*pl.* judud)	new
madĭna (*pl.* mudun)	city
mā' (*pl.* miyāh)	water
akh (*pl.* ikhwat)	brother (*but* ikhwān, brethren)
matā?	when?
ayna?	where?
mashā	to walk

Unit 5

wazîr (*pl.* wuzarā')	minister
kam?	how much?
qad	(verbal particle to indicate the past)
zāra	to visit
li'anna	because
kadhālika	so
abu (*pl.* ābā')	father (of)
Muslim (*pl.* Muslimūn)	Muslim
hāl (*pl.* ahwāl)	health, condition
man?	who?
sabāh, subh	morning
jamî'	all, every, whole
'indamā	when
jarîda (*pl.* jarā'id)	newspaper
bisabab	because
ibn, bin (*pl.* abnā', banūn)	son (of)
Islām	Islam
walad (*pl.* awlād)	son, child, boy
kamā	as
shā'a	to wish

Unit 6

hubb	love
lammā	when
duwalî	international
dhahaba	to go (dhahaba bi, to take away)
hādhir	present
umm (*pl.* ummhāt)	mother
al-bārih, al-bāriha	yesterday
qāma	to rise, stand up, (qāma bi, carry out)
watanî	national
khidma (*pl.* khadamāt)	service
amkana	to be possible
jum'a (*pl.* juma')	week
shāi	tea
mamnū'a	forbidden
harr	hot, heat
khāssa, khusūsan	especially
ākhir (*pl.* awākhir)	last
khārij	outside
hattā	until
salām, silm	peace (greeting)

Unit 7

kataba	to write
khayr	better
āl	family, house
nūr (pl. anwār)	light
masa' (pl. amsīya)	evening
mundhu	since
bikhusūs	concerning
ghāli	expensive
jumhūrīyya	republic
ra'īs (pl. ru'ūsā)	leader, president
ammā.. fa...	as for...
nahnu	we
malaka	to own, possess
kalama	to speak
waqt (pl. awqāt)	time
ayyi?	which?, what?
fulūs (s. fils)	money
fataha	to open, conquer
hutayl	hotel
balad, balda (pl. bilād)	town
antunna	you (f. pl.)

Unit 8

illa	except
sharq	east
Qur'ān	Koran
bahr (*pl.* buhūr, bihār)	sea
awsat	middle
imtalaka	to possess, own
rakhīs	cheap
saghīr (*pl.* sighār)	small, little
talaba (min)	to request (from)
qadīm (*pl.* qudamā')	old
akala	to eat
shāri' (*pl.* shawāri')	road, street
tawīl (*pl.* tiwāl)	long, tall
akhīr	last, latest
jalasa	to sit
qasīr (*pl.* qisār)	short
'amila ('alā)	to do, work (on)
bint, ibna (*pl.* banāt)	girl, daughter (of)
qahwa (*pl.* qahawi)	coffee

Unit 9

bāb (*pl.* abwāb) — door, gate

qasr (*pl.* qusūr) — palace, fort

akhadha — to take, begin

tal'a' — to go out, up

zaman (*pl.* azmān); zamān (*pl.* azmina) — time

'arafa — to know

karīm (*pl.* kiram, kuramā') — noble

kātaba — to correspond with

qalīl (*pl.* qalīlūn, qilāl) — few, little

ahl (*pl.* ahālin, ahlūna) — people, family

ba'īd — far

watan (*pl.* awtān) — homeland

sadīq (*pl.* asdiqā') — friend

ahmar (*pl.* humr) — red

as-Sayyid (*pl.* as-Sādat) — Mr, gentleman

fa'ala — to make, do

jama'a — to gather

sana (*pl.* sinūn, sanawāt) — year

'ālam (*pl.* 'awālim, 'ālūm) — world

jalīl (*pl.* ajilla) — great, important

Unit 10

jā'a	to come (jā'a bi, to bring)
azraq (*pl.* zurq)	blue
kitāb (*pl.* kutub)	book
'ayn (*dual* 'aynayn, *pl.* 'uyūn)	eye, spring
jamīl	beautiful
sahîh (*pl.* sihāh, asha')	healthy, right
ākhar (*f.* ukhrā)	an(other)
qawî (*pl.* aqwiyā')	strong
sha'b (*pl.* shu'ūb)	people
sāra	to go, travel, happen, become
bilād (*pl.* buldān)	country
hadîqa (*pl.* hadā'iq)	garden
qadima	to come, arrive
ukht (*pl.* akhawāt)	sister
nadara (ilā)	to look (at)
shabb (*pl.* shabāb, shubbān)	young man
qarîb (min) (*pl.* aqribā')	near (to), relative
imra'a (*pl.* nisā', niswa, niswān)	woman
sāhib (*pl.* ashāb)	owner
hāza	to get, obtain

Unit 11

law	if
qism (*pl.* aqsām)	part
arāda	to wish
ahyānan	sometimes
hayy (*pl.* ahyā')	alive
sūq (*pl.* aswāq)	market
wajaha	to meet, face
marra	to pass
'āqil	intelligent
siyāsī (*pl.* sāsā, siyāsīyūn)	political, politician
shadīd (*pl.* shidād)	strong
qānūn (*pl.* qawānīn)	law
markaz (*pl.* marākiz)	centre, headquarters
thaqīl (*pl.* thuqalā', thiqāl)	heavy
marra (*dual* marratayn, twice)	time, once
arsala	to send
da'a	to pray, invite
wasala (ilā)	to arrive (at)
tālib (*pl.* tullāb, talaba)	student
zujāj	glass
aswad	black

Unit 12

asmā	to name
hasan	good, handsome
wajada	to find
dhakara	to mention
sābiq	previous
mawt	death
ista'mala	to use
sālim	safe, secure
bulĩs	police
wajaba 'alā	to be incumbent upon
hafla (*pl.* hafalāt)	party
tayib	excellent
qalam (*pl.* aqlām)	pen
waraq (*pl.* awrāq)	paper, card
takallama	to speak
shakl (*pl.* ashkāl)	form, shape
mahatta	shop, station
'atā	to give
qabila	to accept
sālih	sound, honest

Unit 13

rasmī	official
tarīq (*pl.* turuq)	way, road
akhdar (*pl.* khudr)	green
bal	but
asbaha	to become, begin
'ilm (*pl.* 'ulūm)	science
sahha	health, rightness
nataja (min)	to result (from)
'adda	to count
ajnabī (*pl.* ajānib)	foreign(er)
sahl (*pl.* suhūl)	easy
ka +	like, as
ism (*pl.* asmā')	name
ghanī (*pl.* aghniyā)	rich
shahr (*pl.* ashhur, shuhūr)	month
kharaja	to leave, go out
shakka (fī)	to doubt
wasi'a	to be capable of, to be wide
jazīra (*pl.* juzur, al-jazā'ir)	island (al-Jazā'ir, Algeria; Jazīrat al-'arabīyya, Arabian Peninsula)
hawālī	about, approximately
birka (*pl.* birak)	pool

Unit 14

sa'b (*pl.* si'āb)	difficult
mawdū' (*pl.* mawādi')	subject
baynamā	while
shughl (*pl.* ashghāl)	work
taqrîban	almost
laysa	is not
hîna	when
mithl	as, such as
'abr	across
shams (*pl.* shumūs)	sun
'āmala	to deal with
bārid	cold (*adj.*)
mā zāla	to continue, still
'āda	to return
lidhālika	so, therefore
taraka	to leave
hayawān	animal
daraba	to strike, beat
mufîd	useful
'āmm	general

Unit 15

muwaddif	employé
khabar (*pl.* akhbār)	news
adāra	to administer, manage
labisa	to wear
shurta	police
tarīqa (*pl.* tarā'iq, turuq)	way, manner
lam	did not (+ jussive)
dirāsa	study
tabīb (*pl.* atibbā')	doctor
kallama	to speak (to)
'aql (*pl.* 'uqul)	intelligence
tifl (*pl.* atfāl)	child
mushkila (*pl.* mashākil)	problem
qadara ('alā)	to be able to
hasala	to happen (hasala 'alā, to obtain)
waqa'a	to happen, fall
hakadhā	in the same way
sa'ala	to ask
latīf (*pl.* litāf, lutfā)	pleasant, kind
milh	salt

Unit 16

'amal (*pl.* 'amād)	work
jayid (*pl.* jiyād)	good, fine
mawqif (*pl.* mawāqif)	situation
hadatha	to happen
majlis (*pl.* majālis)	council, board
marîd (*pl.* marda)	sick
a'dîm (*pl.* udamā', idām)	great
mat'am (*pl.* matā'im)	restaurant
danna	to think
rasūl (*pl.* rusul)	messenger
khubz	bread
khādim (*pl.* khadam, khuddām)	servant
hadara	to be present at
ustādh (*pl.* asātidha)	teacher, professor
daqîqa (*pl.* daqā'iq)	minute
al-mar'a	womankind
ra'îsî	principal, leading
sabab (*pl.* asbāb)	reason
'ilāqa	relation(ship)
adraka	to realise

Unit 17

raja'a	to return
nahār	daytime
darasa	to study
quwwa	strength
haqq (*pl.* huqūq)	truth, right
sharaba	to drink
da'īf (*pl.* du'fa', di'āf)	weak
māta	to die
ard	earth
ta'ashshā	to dine
dukkān (*pl.* dakākīn)	shop
qatala	to kill
fā'ida (*pl.* fawā'id)	benefit
bahatha	to study, discuss (bahatha 'an, to search for)
'ajīb	marvellous
ghanam (*pl.* aghnām)	sheep
mayyit, mayt (*pl.* mawtā, amwāt)	dead
thawb (*pl.* thīyāb)	robe
madda	to spread
nazala	to come down, go down, stay

Unit 18

gharb	west
ghayr, ghayr anna	non-, not, however
'īd (*pl.* a'yād)	festival
dakhala	to enter
i'taqada	to believe
as-sayyida	Mrs
dahara	to seem
waraqa	piece of paper, card
hadīth	modern, new
shābba	young woman
fallāh	peasant, fellah
'ādil (*pl.* 'adl)	just
aruzz, ruzz	rice
bayd	eggs
'allama	to teach
insān (*pl.* nās, unās)	person, human
muhimm	important
tājir (*pl.* tujjār)	merchant
khusūsī	special, private
finjān (*pl.* fanājīn)	cup

Unit 19

sami'a	to hear
qawm (*pl.* aqwām)	race, people, nation
qissa (*pl.* qisas)	story
wasat (*pl.* awsāt)	middle
bank (*pl.* bunūk)	bank
barīd	post
mintaqa (*pl.* manātiq)	district
'arada	to offer, show
haraka	movement
bayān (*pl.* bayānāt)	statement (al-bayān, the Qur'ān)
qasama	to divide
jam'īyya	association
Misr	Egypt
iblagha	to inform
iqtisād	economy
a'jaba	to surprise
sabaqa	to precede
hadd (*pl.* hudūd)	frontier, limit
samaha (bi) ... li	to grant (to), permit ... to
lugha	language

Unit 20

mathalan	for instance
amr (*pl.* umūr)	matter, affairs, order, (but *pl.* awāmir, orders)
lan	will not (with subjunctive)
rafa'a	to raise
ad-duhr	midday
maskan (*pl.* masākin)	dwelling
hāwala	to try, attempt
khatar (*pl.* akhtār)	danger
banā	to build
'ām (*pl.* a'wām)	year
qara'a	to read
natīja (*pl.* natā'ij)	result
khayr	good, welfare
sana'a	to make, manufacture
antaja	to produce
ma'qūl	intelligent
'adad (*pl.* a'dād)	number
kalām	talk, discourse
naw' (*pl.* anwā')	sort, type
da'a (ilā)	to call (for)

Unit 21

sharika	company
sallama bi	to accept (sallama ... ilā, to hand over ... to; sallama 'alā, to greet)
'askarĭ (*pl.* 'asākir, 'askar)	soldier
idāra	administration
zara'a	to cultivate
kay, likay	in order to
naft	oil (mineral)
bilqurbi min	near
hā'it (*pl.* haytān)	wall
taghaddā	to take lunch
haqqaqa	to achieve (*but* haqqaqa fĭ, to investigate)
hĭn (*pl.* ahyān)	time
intadara	to wait (for)
halla	to settle, solve
nahr (*pl.* anhār, anhur)	river
hatta	to put down
mudĭr	manager
maslaha (*pl.* masālih)	welfare, interest
fahima	to understand
wahda (*pl.* wahadāt)	unity

Unit 22

wara'a	behind
maftūh	open
hādith (*pl.* hawādith)	event, accident
ayyî	that is, i.e.
mithāl (*pl.* amthila)	example
hizb (*pl.* ahzāb)	party, group
madrasa (*pl.* madāris)	school
jabal (*pl.* jibāl)	mountain
marad (*pl.* amrād)	illness
rijl (*dual* rijlain, *pl.* arjul)	leg
tijāha	in front of
qābala	to meet
nā'ib (*pl.* nuwwāb)	deputy
haqîqa (*pl.* haqā'iq)	truth
ka's (*pl.* ku'ūs)	glass
lahm (*pl.* luhūm, lihām)	meat
janūb	south
hāla	situation
waffaqa	to help
sāha bi	to call out to

Unit 23

sūra (*pl.* suwar)	picture
yamīn	right
darūrī	necessary
'umr (*pl.* a'mār)	age
siyāsa	politics
khārijī	exterior, external
shakhsīyya	personality
ishtarā	to buy
zawāj	marriage
raqm (*pl.* arqām)	number
yasār	left
sha'n (*pl.* shu'ūn)	thing, matter
mamlaka (*pl.* mamālik)	kingdom
al-mashriq	the East, Orient
a'lana	to advertise, announce
risāla (*pl.* rasā'il, risālāt)	letter
shamāl	north
qamar (*pl.* aqmār)	moon
'alima	to learn, know
qarya (*pl.* qurā)	village

Unit 24

ta'allama	to learn
dūna	without
balāgh (*pl.* balāghāt)	report
muhandis	engineer
wafd (*pl.* wufūd)	delegation
sarafa	to spend
amīn (*pl.* amanā')	faithful, secretary
mana'a	to prohibit
'ashā'	dinner
bid', bid'a	a few
firāsh	bed
ma'rifa (*pl.* ma'ārif)	(realms of) knowledge
ta'ām (*pl.* at'ima)	food
bada'a	to start
sur'a	speed
qadam (*dual* qadamain, *pl.* aqdām)	foot
sāfara	to travel
sabī (*pl.* sibya, sibyān)	boy
yad (*dual* yadain, *pl.* aydin)	hand
faras (*pl.* afrās)	horse, mare

Unit 25

jānib (*pl.* jawānib)	side
radī' (*pl.* ardiyā')	bad
jamal (*pl.* jimāl)	camel
samak (*pl.* asmāk)	fish
badawî (*pl.* badu, badawîyyūn)	nomad, beduin
abdā	to show
ladā	at, near, by
shart (*pl.* shurūt)	condition
akhbara bi ('an)	to inform of (about)
hāmm	important
dayyiq	narrow
'umūmî	public, general
hulw	sweet
'azîz (*pl.* 'aizza')	dear
basît (*pl.* busatā)	simple
badā	to seem
ghada'	luncheon
mahall (*pl.* mahāll, mahallāt)	place
adraba	to go on strike
qata'a	to cut

Unit 26

raml (*pl.* rimāl)	sand
'ahd (*pl.* 'uhūd)	contract, promise
anshā'	to establish
handasa	engineering
lawn (*pl.* alwān)	colour
qātala	to fight
ra'y (*pl.* arā')	opinion
wājib (*pl.* wājibāt)	duty
madanī	civil, civilian
salīm (*pl.* sulamā')	safe, secure
wāli (*pl.* wulāt)	governor
kalima	word
shajar, shajara (*pl.* ashjār, shajarāt)	tree
mu'allim (*f.* mu'allima)	teacher (*m.*)
'ā'idāt, 'awā'id	profits
bā'a	to sell
aqāma	to set up, raise
dākhilī	interior, internal
fakkara fī	to consider
atāha li	to permit

Unit 27

bāhatha ... fī	to discuss ... with
darūra	need
bustān (*pl.* basātîn)	orchard
sadara	to be issued
wakîl (*pl.* wukalā')	deputy, agent
dars (*pl.* durūs)	lesson
amina	to be safe, secure
di'āya	propaganda
taqsîm	division
aththara 'alā, fī	to influence
'abd (*pl.* 'abîd, 'ibād)	slave
harrara	to liberate, edit
khafîf (*pl.* akhfāf, akhiffā', khifāf)	light (in weight)
aftara	to breakfast
lisān (*pl.* alsina, alsun)	tongue
istafāda (min)	to benefit (from)
mashhūr (bi)	famous (for)
sarî'	quick
aslî	original
'ajiba bi	to admire

Unit 28

tārīkh (*pl.* tawārīkh)	date, history
darf (*pl.* durūf)	circumstance
sinā'a	industry
'idda	a number (of)
wāsita (*pl.* wasā'it)	means
'allaqa ('alā)	to comment (on), to hang (on to)
qawmī	nationalist
'āsima (*pl.* 'awāsim)	capital
husn	goodness
umma (*pl.* umam)	nation
markab (*pl.* marākib)	ship
lahda	moment
istaqbala	to receive
sawt (*pl.* aswāt)	voice, vote
mazra'a (*pl.* mazari')	farm, plantation
walāsīyyamā	especially
hawla	about, around
zayt (*pl.* zuyūt)	oil
hasaba	to calculate
tanawwa'	to be varied

Unit 29

makan (*pl.* amākin, amkina)	place
hādatha	to converse
limā, limādhā	why?
funduq (*pl.* fanādiq)	hotel
'asrî	modern
tāra	to fly
'anā	to mean
ghadiba ('alā)	to be angry (with)
'imāra	building
wilāya	province
jaww (*pl.* ajwā')	air, weather
barlamān	Parliament
wassa'a	to widen (*trans.*)
jarā	to happen, run
'adl	justice
wahhada	to unify
tazawwaja	to marry
daraja	step, degree
mu'āsir	contemporary
daqîq (*pl.* diqāq)	accurate, fine, thin

Unit 30

ahabba	to love
tahassana	to improve (*intrans.*)
wajh (*pl.* awjuh, wujūh)	face. surface
ashā'	to spread (news) (*trans.*)
nidām (*pl.* andima)	system, order
sinā'ī	artificial
'abara	to cross
fikra (*pl.* afkār, fikar)	idea
ishtaghala	to work
tasrīh (*pl.* tasrīhāt)	permission, declaration
naffadha	to carry out
'āla	tool
hakama	to rule
bādiya (*pl.* bawādin)	desert
ijtimā'ī	social
sāna	to protect
matar (*pl.* amtār)	rain
hawa'	air, wind
hāja	thing, necessity
tawwara	to develop (*trans.*)

Unit 31

adāfa (ilā)	to add
gharîb (*pl.* ghurabā')	strange(r)
qā'ima (*pl.* qāwā'im, qā'imāt)	list
wathiqa (bi)	to trust
sāhil (*pl.* sawāhil)	coast, shore
hamala ('alā)	to carry (to attack)
ishtaraka (fî)	to share (in), participate (in)
zawj (*pl.* azwāj)	husband
balagha	to reach, amount to
qā'id (*pl.* qāda, quwwād)	general, leader
jumhur (*pl.* jamāhîr)	crowd, public
nāba ('an)	to deputise (for)
mathl (*pl.* amthāl)	proverb
mudda (*pl.* mudad)	period
ghurfa (*pl.* ghuraf)	room
khilāl	during
maktab (*pl.* makātib)	office
dāfa'a ('an)	to defend
wādih	clear
'alaja	to deal with

Unit 32

yadawî	manual
ahdatha	to create, cause
qādim	next
darrasa	to teach
nār (*f., pl.* nîrān)	fire
baqara (*pl.* baqarāt)	cow (*but* baqar, *pl.* cattle)
fitr, fatūr	breakfast
tayr (*pl.* tuyūr)	bird
sanawî	annual
amara	to order
hālan	at once
awqafa	to stop (*trans.*)
Urūba	Europe
mablagh (*pl.* mabāligh)	amount
mā'ida (*pl.* mā'idat, mawā'id)	table
fākiha (*pl.* fawākih)	fruit
riyāl (*pl.* riyālāt)	riyal
qalb (*pl.* qulūb)	heart
asmar (*pl.* sumr)	brown
mawsim (*pl.* mawāsim)	season

Unit 33

jazīlan	very much
idhā	if
nakhl	palm trees
haythu	since
tawajjaha	to go towards
sahāfa	press, journalism
suhūla	ease
'amīq	deep
su'āl (*pl.* as'ila)	question
ijtama'a	to meet
aqada	to tie, contract
matara	to rain
istiqlāl	independence
mujtahid	industrious
shidda	strength
nadīf (*pl.* niddāf)	clean
qit'a (*pl.* qita', qit'āt)	piece
ta'bān	tired
tuffāh	apples
i'tazala	to retire

Unit 34

asl (*pl.* usūl)	origin
wāsi'	wide
bijānibi	beside
tabbākh	cook
jāwara	to adjoin
akhīran	finally
atamma	to complete
wikāla	agency
amāma	in front of
aslaha	to reform
mas'ūl ('an)	responsible (for)
wāfaqa ('alā)	to agree (with)
nashara	to publish
malika	queen
dawla (*pl.* duwal)	state
sath (*pl.* sutūh, astiha)	surface
farīq (*pl.* furaqā')	team
'udwu (*pl.* a'dā')	member
khabir (*pl.* khubarā') bi	expert (on)
dhaki (*pl.* adhkiyā')	clever

Unit 35

tatawwara	to develop (*intrans.*)
hukm (*pl.* ahkām)	order
khayl, khuyūl (*both pl.*)	horses
dalla ('alā)	to point to
Ifrīqiyah	Africa
hāli	present (*adj.*)
irtafa'a	to rise
ahammīyya	importance
tamma	to be complete
saddara	to export
mar'	human being
rākib (*pl.* rukkāb)	passenger
wad' (*pl.* awda')	situation
wālid (*f.* wālida)	parent; father, mother
su'ūba	difficulty
makhraj	exit
asfar (*pl.* sufr)	yellow
ijtimā'	meeting
nashā'	to grow
zubda	butter

Unit 36

hafada ('alā)	to protect
sallaha	to repair
khāfa	to fear
mawdi' (*pl.* mawādi')	place
rakiba	to ride, embark
fasl (*pl.* fusūl)	chapter
ijtahada	to work hard
hasiba	to support
nashīt	active
hisān (*pl.* ahsina, husun)	horse
zawja	wife
thawra	revolution
khibra (*pl.* khubr)	experience
naqala	to transport
mandūb	delegate
wasikh	dirty
hākim (*pl.* hukkām)	ruler
nashra (*pl.* nasharāt)	publication
murr	bitter
'anīf	violent

Unit 37

mahkama (*pl.* mahākim)	court
in	if
hassana	to improve (*trans.*)
mādda (*pl.* mawāddu)	substance
juz' (*pl.* ajzā')	part
hamā	to protect
ajrā	to carry out
safīna (*pl.* sufun)	ship
maththala	to represent
mādī, al-mādī	past, the past
jubn, jubna	cheese
lazima	to be necessary
khadama	to serve
azma (*pl.* azamāt)	crisis
dābit (*pl.* dubbāt)	office
sādir (*pl.* sādirāt)	export
ibtada'a	to start
fātih	light-coloured
ihtāja (ilā)	to need
hamla (*pl.* hamalāt)	attack (*n.*)

Unit 38

ra'ā	to see
nahwa	towards, about
nisf (*pl.* ansāf)	half
fannî	artistic, technical
harb (*f. pl.* hurūb)	war
sākin (*pl.* sukkān)	inhabitant
haddada	to (de)limit
mahabba	love
fursa (*pl.* furas)	occasion
assasa	to found
sāqa	to drive
itla'a	to inform of
mā (lā) ... abadan	never
matbakh (*pl.* matābikh)	kitchen
amîr (*pl.* umarā')	Emir, Prince
qarrara	to decide (to)
difā'	defence
zāda	to increase
dayf (*pl.* duyūf)	guest
asra'a	to hurry

Unit 39

amn, amān	security
safar (*pl.* asfār)	journey
masna' (*pl.* masāni')	factory
qatīl (*pl.* qitli)	killed
madkhal	entrance
ghā'ib	absent
maktaba	library, bookshop
jāwaba	to answer
baladīyya	municipality
'ālim (*pl.* 'ulamā')	scientist, scholar
ithnā'	during
waqafa	to stop (waqafa 'alā, to understand)
nā'ib (*pl.* nuwwāb)	deputy
tamr (*pl.* tumūr)	date
hisāb (*pl.* hisābāt)	account
hadīth (*pl.* ahādīth)	talk
haya	to live
fattasha	to inspect
'ādatan	usually
athara (*pl.* āthār)	trace, antiquities

Unit 40

allafa	to compose, write
masrūf (*pl.* masārif)	expenditure
adhara	to show
asās (*pl.* usus)	foundation
jaysh (*pl.* juyūsh)	army
mashghūl	busy
dā'ira (*pl.* dawā'ir)	office
zirā'a	agriculture
mustaqbil	future
radda ('alā)	to return, reply
inkasara	to be broken
'ārada	to oppose
sahīfa	newspaper (*pl.* suhuf, press)
manzil (*pl.* manāzil)	residence
shamila	to comprise
sundūq (*pl.* sanādīq)	box
thalj (*pl.* thulūj)	ice, snow
qīma (*pl.* qiyam)	value
hurr (*pl.* ahrār)	free
akhraja	to expel, remove

Unit 41

tafaddala 'alā	to be so good as to
jāmi' (*pl.* jawāmi')	mosque
nisba (*pl.* nisab)	relation
istarāha	to rest
rafīq (*pl.* rufaqā')	companion
usbū' (*pl.* asābi')	week
sharrafa	to honour
majmū'	total
jawāb (*pl.* ajwiba)	answer
'adū (*pl.* a'dā')	enemy
radd	reply
mudhik	funny
muhālafa	alliance
ajāba	to answer
badhala	to strive
'ā'ila (*pl.* 'awā'il, 'ā'ilāt)	family
jihād	holy war
dahika ('alā, min)	to laugh (at)
tasarrafa	to behave
farhān (*pl.* farhā)	happy

Unit 42

istama'a (ilā)	to listen (to)
ghanna	to sing
majalla	magazine
da'wa (*pl.* da'awāt)	claim, invitation
ijāza	vacation, permission
khassa	to concern
masjid (*pl.* masājid)	mosque
kasara	to break
masrif (*pl.* masārif)	bank
jawāz safar (*pl.* jawazāt safar)	passport
tawassala ilā	to reach
'arīd	wide
siyāha	tourism
khazana	to store
taba'a	to print
i'tarafa (bi)	to acknowledge, admit
maqāl, maqāla (*pl.* maqālāt)	article (journalism)
haddara	to prepare, make ready
mas'a	effort
rāha	rest

Unit 43

'asr (*pl.* 'asur, 'usūr)	time, late afternoon
intahā	to end
ashara (ilā)	to indicate, point (to)
fata (*pl.* fityān)	young man
ta'āwana (ma'a)	to cooperate (with)
si'r (*pl.* as'ār)	price
harasa	to guard
jār (*pl.* jîrān)	neighbour
rîh (*pl.* riyāh)	wind
nāqasha	to argue with
mustashfā (*pl.* mustashfayāt)	hospital
jamal	beauty
îjār	hire
sā'in (*pl.* su'āt)	messenger
tabî'î	natural
tafsîl (*pl.* tafāsîl, tafsîlāt)	detail
qarār (*pl.* qarārāt)	decision
wathîq (*pl.* withāq)	firm, trustworthy
sajjāda (*pl.* sajājîd)	carpet
'ayyana	to appoint

Unit 44

ammā ... aw	either ... or
sahrā' (*pl.* sahārā)	desert
tadhkira (*pl.* tadhākir)	ticket
tamāman	completely
āsif	sorry
nādi (*pl.* andīya)	club
rabiha	to win
dhātu	the same
la'iba	to play
ma'āsh (*pl.* ma'āshāt)	wages
adab (*pl.* ādāb)	literature
khallā	to leave
tashakkara li ('alā)	to be grateful to (for)
masaka	to hold, grasp
dhahab	gold
sawwara	to photograph, draw
nasiya	to forget
rakada	to run
thaqāfa	culture
qabr (*pl.* qubūr)	grave

Unit 45

qarîban	soon
'amalî	practical
rihla	journey
sikkîn (*pl.* sakākîn)	knife
kullîyya	college, faculty
iqtasara 'alā	to be confined to
nāla	to obtain
dāma	to last
mumtāz	excellent
qabada	to grip, take hold of (qabada 'alā, to seize)
ittala'a 'alā	to be informed of
kursî (*pl.* karāsî)	chair
mitr (*pl.* amtār)	metre
jami'a	university
shakara ('alā)	to thank (for)
ma'mal (*pl.* ma'āmil)	factory
mahdūd	limited
dîn (*pl.* adyān)	religion
ghayyara	to change (*trans.*)
'āsha	to live

Unit 46

sahn (*pl.* suhūn)	plate
mahallī	local
hadīd	iron, steel
nāma	to sleep
rātib (*pl.* rawātib)	salary
tawaqqa'a	to expect
ahdara	to bring, fetch
faddala ... ('alā)	to prefer ... (to)
nadarī	theoretical
bināya	building
istatā'a	to be able
intabaha ilā	to notice
sadda	to close
māl (*pl.* amwāl)	wealth, property
madanīyya	civilisation
mawqi' (*pl.* mawāqi')	place
nuskha (*pl.* nusakh)	copy
banzīn	petrol
kharraba	to destroy
imtihān	examination

Unit 47

rubbamā	perhaps
kīlū	kilogramme
ahamma	to be of interest
dirham (*pl.* darāhim)	dirham (currency)
ma'nā (*pl.* ma'ānin)	meaning
'iwādan 'an	instead of
wāqi'a (*pl.* waqā'i')	incident
nabbaha ilā	to call attention to
sadāqa	friendship
ruh (*pl.* arwāh)	spirit
matār (*pl.* matārāt)	airport
kāmil	complete
iftakara	to think
sābiqan	previously
'inda'dhan	at that time
fard (*pl.* afrād)	individual
mathaf (*pl.* matāhif)	museum
jalī	clear
bisur'a	quickly
ra's (*pl.* ru'ūs)	head

Unit 48

'aks   contrary ('alā 'l-'aksi, on the contrary)

nihāya   end (*n.*)

adhā'a   to broadcast

kilūmitr   kilometre

jā'i' (*pl.* jiyā')   hungry

qitār   train

ajjāra (li)   to lease (to)

dalāla (*pl.* dalā'il)   direction, indication

maydān (*pl.* mayādin)   square, field

nasaha   to advise

rattaba   to arrange

wijdān   consciousness

tibqan li   according to

hani'   pleasant

akrama   to honour

baghtatan   suddenly

hadiya (*pl.* hadāyā)   gift

irād   income

barnāmaj (*pl.* barāmij)   program(me)

rasama   to draw

Unit 49

tarjama	to translate
tabi'a	to follow
masīhī	Christian
ma'īsha	means of life
'ammara	to develop
tafawwaqa 'alā	to surpass
mustawī	standard
dahr (*pl.* duhūr)	back
dahisha	to be surprised
mabda' (*pl.* mabāda')	principle
kasaba	to gain, earn
qarn (*pl.* qurūn)	horn, century
nuqta (*pl.* niqāt, nuqat)	point
istawrada	to import
ghalat, ghalta (*pl.* aghlāt)	mistake
warada	to arrive
kahrabā', kahrubā'	electricity
anfaqa	to spend
munāsaba	occasion
iktashafa	to discover

Unit 50

hāris (*pl.* hurrās)	guard
sathī	superficial
sakana (ilā)	to inhabit (to be content with)
murīh	comfortable
jadd (*pl.* ajdād, judūd)	grandfather
farq (*pl.* furūq)	difference
jadīr (bi)	worthy (of)
'ama (*pl.* u'mī)	blind
ikhtabara	to experience
qutn (*pl.* aqtān)	cotton
nāsaba	to suit, be related to
dīwān (*pl.* dawāwīn)	office, settee, poetry anthology
adāt (*pl.* adawāt)	tool
inbasata	to enjoy oneself
absara	to see
nafaqa	expense
far' (*pl.* furū')	branch
hālaman	as soon as
ista'dhana	to ask permission
khatama	to seal, conclude

Unit 51

taghayyara	to be changed
'āqiba (*pl.* 'awāqib)	result
awjada	to create
rutba (*pl.* rutab)	rank, class
yanbaghí li	it is incumbent on
liss (*pl.* lusūs)	thief
'amalíyya	operation
hatab	firewood
dakhm	huge
makhfar (*pl.* makhāfir)	police post
wasafa	to describe
muhādara	lecture
ikhsā'í	specialist
infasala ('an)	to separate (from)
khazzān	dam, reservoir
junayh	pound (currency)
ba'atha	to send
haddād	smith
'āqaba (bi, 'alā)	to punish (for)
amdā	to sign

Unit 52

shāhada	to witness
fahasa	to examine
ijtāza	to cross
tabī'a (*pl.* tabā'i')	nature
waqqa'a	to sign
dīnār (*pl.* dinānīr)	dinar (currency)
irtāha (li, ilā)	to be pleased (with)
'arrafa (bi)	to inform, acquaint (with)
nadaran li, ilā	in view of
thā'ir (*pl.* thuwwār)	rebel
fadlan 'an	apart from
sa'ā (ilā)	to strive (to)
haqqan	really
ihtarasa (min)	to be on guard (against)
ghalita	to be mistaken
khafīr (*pl.* khufarā')	watchman
Sūriyyā	Syria
idhan	therefore
muwātin	citizen
ghādara	to depart from

Unit 53

'unwān (*pl.* 'anāwîn)	address
innamā	just, only
ghāliban	generally
ma'an	together
raghiba	to desire, wish
wāridāt	imports
kāda	to be almost
marsūm (*pl.* marāsîm)	decree
rabata (bi)	to tie (to)
rasm (*pl.* rusūm)	drawing
istaqāla	to resign
martaba (*pl.* marātib)	class, order
dhati-	self
'āda (*pl.* 'adāt, 'awā'id)	custom
idh	since
'utla (*pl.* 'utal)	holiday
basata	to explain
fatāt (*pl.* fatyāt)	young woman
madā	to proceed
walia	to take office, follow

Unit 54

mandar	view (*pl.* manādir, landscape)
haqīqatan	really
fann (*pl.* funūn)	art, technology
sifāra	embassy
qutr (*pl.* aqtār)	region
afāda	to be useful
wāsala	to continue
matbū'āt	printed matter
ihtamala	to endure
ughniyya (*pl.* aghānī, āghāni)	song
'āli	high
tasawwara	to imagine
ma'hid (*pl.* ma'āhid)	institute
i'tadā 'alā	to attack
makhzan (*pl.* makhāzin)	store
insarafa	to go away
farah	happiness
ta'arrafa ('alā, bi)	to become acquainted (with)
awdaha	to make clear
istamarra	to continue

Important Message

Please read the instruction booklet carefully. If you experience any difficulty in operating your Slim-Gym there is no need to return the product. Simply call our helpline and ask for Ann Roberts who will be able to give advice and assistance.

Customer Helpline 01242-250443

Unit 55

intasaba ilā	to be related to
tāqa	power, energy
mawrid (*pl.* mawārid)	resource
jumla (*pl.* jumal)	sentence
za'ama	to assert, pretend
idhn	permission
al-ishtirākīyya	socialism
tafāhama	to understand each other
qārana bi	to compare with
waqti'dhin	at that time
thaqqafa	to educate
falsafa	philosophy
jawharī	essential
kashafa	to uncover (kashafa 'alā, to examine)
fakka	to separate
hīna'dhin	then
karam	generosity
addā (ilā)	to pay, lead (to)
wifqan li	in accordance with
sikkat hadīd (*pl.* sikak hadīd)	railway

Unit 56

matlab (*pl.* matālib)	request
karama	honour (*n.*)
mas'ala (*pl.* masā'il)	question, problem
'athara ('alā)	to come across
muzāri'	farmer
rāfaqa	to accompany
ikhtalafa 'an	to differ from
'āmil (*pl.* 'awāmil)	factor
nadarīyya	theory
in'akasa	to be reflected
ba'da'dhin	afterwards
nafiqa	to be spent
'amada li, ilā	to intend to
tābiq (*pl.* tawābiq)	storey
sha'ara	to feel (sha'ara ma'a, to sympathise)
sukkar	sugar
fadl (*pl.* afdāl, fudūl)	favour
shakk (*pl.* shukūk)	doubt
khitām	conclusion
dill (*pl.* adlāl, dilāl)	shadow
tābi' (*pl.* tawābi')	postage stamp

Unit 57

sikritīr	secretary
mustaqīm	straight
dam (*pl.* dima')	blood
sā'iq	driver
kammīyya	quantity
damina	to guarantee
sāmin	high
usbu', isba' (*pl.* asābi')	finger
sarraha (bi)	to permit, declare
ikhtassa bi	to belong to, specialise in
binā' (*pl.* anbīya)	building
baddala	to change
rābita (*pl.* rawābit)	tie
qādi (*pl.* qudāt)	judge
fāwada	to negotiate
dustūr (*pl.* dasātīr)	constitution
tajāwaza	to exceed
wathīqa (*pl.* wathā'iq)	document, archives
sādiq	honest
shaddada	to strengthen (shaddada 'alā, to emphasise)

Unit 58

khatir	dangerous
shahida	to testify, be present at
dabbara	to arrange
jisr (*pl.* jusūr)	bridge
a'āna	to help
juhd (*pl.* judūd)	ability
miskîn (*pl.* masākîn)	poor
qā'ida (*pl.* qawā'id)	rule
ghadbān (*pl.* ghidāb)	angry
istaradda	to recover
tā'ira	aircraft
khutwa	step
wahîd	unique
ma'nawî	mental, abstract
himma (*pl.* himam)	energy
ba'tha (*pl.* ba'athāt)	mission
fassala	to detail
hazîn (*pl.* hazana, hizān)	sad
jā'a	to be hungry
marhala (*pl.* marāhil)	stage (of journey)

Unit 59

sharīf (*pl.* ashrāf, shurafā')	noble
akl	food
muqbil	forthcoming
jundī (*pl.* junūd)	soldier
mu'akhkhiran	lately
bā'ith, bā'itha (*pl.* bawā'ith)	motive, purpose
rāqaba	to observe
bi'r (*pl.* ābār)	well
taqaddama	to precede, progress
jadda (*pl.* jaddāt)	grandmother
sajjala	to record
hayāt	life
nā'im	soft
jadura (bi)	to be worthy (of)
muharrir	editor
mufattish	inspector
amāna	fidelity, secretariat
da'wa (*pl.* da'āwā, da'āwin)	lawcase, claim
hurrīyya	freedom
sā'ih (*pl.* siyyāh)	tourist

Unit 60

mu'tadil	moderate
baraka	blessing
tadāhara	to demonstrate
qal'a (*pl.* qilā')	fortress
wasf (*pl.* awsāf)	description
halîb	milk
idtaraba	to be disturbed
anhā	to finish
raghba (*pl.* raghabāt)	desire, wish (*n.*)
khasira	to lose
tanfîdhî	executive
irtabata (bi)	to be tied (to)
tilmîdh (*pl.* talāmîdh, talāmidha)	pupil
i'tabara	to consider
'adîd	numerous
nahw (*pl.* anhā')	grammar, method
'abbara 'an	to express
rafada	to refuse
majran (*pl.* majārin)	course

Unit 61

najaha	to succeed
tadbīr (*pl.* tadābīr)	arrangement
kafā	to suffice
talaqqa	to receive
shayyada	to build, construct
rubba	many a ...
atā'a	to obey
alqā ('alā)	to ask a question (of), deliver a speech (to)
ma'rid (*pl.* ma'ārid)	exhibition
jawhar (*pl.* jawāhir)	essence, jewel
karrama	to honour
naqd (*pl.* nuqūd)	cash
mu'dam	most of
rahhaba	to welcome
salafan	in advance
dāra	to turn, rotate (*intrans.*)
khilāfan li	contrary to
ja'ala	to begin, make
maw'id (*pl.* mawā'id)	appointment
hasbamā	according as (fahasbu, only)

Unit 62

baqîyya (*pl.* baqāyā)	rest (*n.*)
bākir	early
majāl (*pl.* majālāt)	scope, field
darb (*pl.* durūb)	path, track
kharūf (*pl.* khirāf, khirfān)	sheep, lamb
maqsid (*pl.* maqāsid)	intent(ion)
miftah (*pl.* mafātîh)	key
ittafaqa ma'a	to agree with
matba'a (*pl.* matābi')	printing press
aghlab	most of
mahsūl (*pl.* mahāsil, mahsulāt)	crop
ikhtāra	to select
safha	page
kaslān (*pl.* kasāli)	idle
sijill	register
laqiya	to meet, find
'aqiba	after
iktafā (bi)	to be satisfied (with)
bukhār	steam
bayyana	to explain

Unit 63

thaman (*pl.* athmān)	price
asdara	to issue
bashar	human being
dalām	darkness
hawwala	to change
maktūb	letter
jalsa (*pl.* jalasāt)	session
jaraha	to wound
murabba'	square
himār (*pl.* hamīr)	donkey
fākhir	magnificent
Amrīkā	America
taraf	side, viewpoint
sawwā	to settle
shaytān (*pl.* shayātīn)	devil
fā'iq	excellent
rajā	to hope, request
'atīq (*pl.* 'utaqā')	antique
bida'a (*pl.* badā")	goods
sajīn (*pl.* sujanā')	prisoner
dīmūqrātīyyu	democratic

Unit 64

kalb (*pl.* kilāb)	dog
zamîl (*pl.* zumala')	colleague
anîs	sociable
dawra	course
wādi (*pl.* awdiya, widyān)	valley, wadi
haffada	to reduce
mustadîr	round
mujtama'a	community
aghlabîyya	majority
khashiya	to fear
sulm (*pl.* salālim)	stairs
istakhbārāt	information
ummama	to nationalise
fadî'	horrible
nawawî	nuclear
bāshara bi	to manage, begin
arjah	probable
muhît	circumference, ocean
khashab (*pl.* akhshāb)	wood
baraza	to emerge

Unit 65

munaddama	organisation
asāba	to be right, hit
sulh	peace
dalīl (*pl.* adlā')	guide(book)
ittasala bi	to be connected with
Āsiyā	Asia
ijrā' (*pl.* ijrā'āt)	action
nāhiyā (*pl.* nawāhin)	direction
sarrāf	money-changer
ānisa	Miss, young woman
tayrān	airline, aviation
shuyū'ī	communist
tahawwala ilā	to be changed into
ibtasama	to smile
dakhl	income
majhūl	unknown
i'tāda	to be used to
muwaqqat, mu'aqqat	temporary
mubāshir	direct
salāma	safety

Unit 66

adhasha	to surprise
kātib (*pl.* kuttāb)	clerk
Maghrib	West, Morocco
faqîr (*pl.* fuqarā')	poor
sabbaba	to cause
'amm (*pl.* 'umuma, a'mām)	paternal uncle
istakhraja	to extract
qaddama	to offer
tamakkana min	to be able to
qumāsh (*pl.* aqmisha)	cloth
hikma	wisdom
jins (*pl.* ajnās)	kind, gender
suhūfi	press (*adj.*)
bi'îr	camels
i'tabāran min	with effect from
zawwada (bi)	to supply (with)
diyāfa	hospitality
khālafa	to disagree (with)
hajama 'alā	to attack
fārigh	empty

Unit 67

istalama	to receive
Īrān	Iran
zaytūn	olives
shahāda	testimony, certificate
khāl (*pl.* akhwāl)	maternal uncle
hādd	sharp
naddafa	to clean
mashrūb	drink
ittasa'a	to be widespread
mu'askar (*pl.* mu'askarāt)	army camp
wajjaha (ilā)	to direct (to)
jāhada	to struggle
taqs (*pl.* tuqūs)	weather
mu'tamar (*pl.* mu'tamarāt)	conference
qiyāda	leadership
tawassata (fī)	to intervene (in), be in the middle (of)
khashin	rough
istalāh	technical term
wudūh	clarity
ta'awwada	to get used to

Unit 68

shakkala	to form
mudlim	dark
shahna (*pl.* shahnāt, shihan)	cargo
thamīn	valuable
jarrāh	surgeon
qa'ada	to sit down
fulān	Mr So-and-so
ījabī	positive
mithāq (*pl.* mawāthīq)	pact
ajbara ('alā)	to force, compel (to)
qadīyya (*pl.* qadāyā)	ease, question
rā'iha (*pl.* rawā'ih)	smell
aktharīyya	majority
'unsurī	racial
sharr (*pl.* shurūr)	evil
farih (*pl.* farhūn)	happy
'atisha	to be thirsty
sarra	to please
baqqāl	greengrocer
nafi'a	to profit, be of benefit to

Unit 69

nitāq (*pl.* nutuq)	extent, zone
ihtafala	to celebrate
hadāra	civilisation
sayf (*pl.* asyāf)	summer
hinta	wheat
atrash (*pl.* tursh)	deaf
wasakh, wasākha (*pl.* awsākh)	dirt, *pl.* trash
sawā	to be equal to
film (*pl.* aflām)	film
baqī	to remain
shurba	soup
ka'anna	as though
ista'rada	to review
banna'	builder
shitā' (*pl.* ashtiya)	winter
akhkhara	to delay
halīf (*pl.* hulafā)	ally
'arīda (*pl.* 'arā'id)	petition
'usfūr (pl. 'usāfir)	small bird
khizāna (*pl.* khazā'in)	cupboard

Unit 70

khārita, kharîta (*pl.* kharā'it)	map, plan
basharî	human
mutakallim	spokesperson
nashifa	to dry off
ista'jara (min)	to hire (from)
istalaha ('alā)	to agree (on)
jamā'a	group
uns	social life
nafā	to deny, exile
fāja'	to come across, surprise
ishtadda	to intensify, become strong
jahila	to be ignorant of
barr	land
intamā ilā	to belong to
sha'îr	barley
mawwala	to finance
mudawwar	round
'azama ('alā)	to determine (to)
wa'ada	to promise
sifa	quality
sāhaba	to accompany
hājama	to attack

Unit 71

makkana ... (min)	to enable... (to)
salahīyya	qualification
wafāh (*pl.* wafayāt)	death
jāmala	to be polite to
ishtamala 'alā	to contain
'awn	help
wadīfa (*pl.* wadā'if)	employment
farīd	unique
fadīla (*pl.* fadā'il)	merit
barrara	to justify
dūlār	dollar
mutawāsil	continuous
'āmil (*pl.* 'amala, 'ummāl)	labourer
za'lān	angry
fajr	dawn
taqlīd (*pl.* taqālīd)	tradition
qiwām	support
tamthīl	representation
safīr (*pl.* sufarā')	ambassador
idtirāb	disturbance

Unit 72

didda	against
ghasala	to wash
lajna (*pl.* lijān)	committee
bālagha fī	to exaggerate
istaghfara	to beg pardon of
ijbārī	compulsory
mahara fī, bi	to be skilled in
sarīh (*pl.* surahā')	clear, candid
adā'a	to lose, waste
sifr (*pl.* asfār)	zero
khada'a	to deceive
iftarada	to suppose
khawwala	to authorise
sharaha	to explain
safh (*pl.* sufūh)	slope
jawla	tour
khalaqa	to create
qāwama	to oppose
'ulū	height
fassara	to explain

Unit 73

'adam	lack
ittaba'a	to follow
'uqūba	punishment
shābaha	to resemble
biwāsita	by means of
suhba	company
i'tana bi	to take care of
balīgh (*pl.* bulaghā')	eloquent
ahlaka	to destroy
murajjah	probable
badan (*pl.* abdān)	body
jiha	side, direction
amala	to hope (for)
mawadda	friendship
aradā	to please
hazīma	defeat
hāla	to prevent
muka"aba	cube
tasallama	to receive
radia	to accept (*but* radia 'an, to be pleased with)

Unit 74

aghlaqa	to shut
murāqib	observer
hāraba	to fight
istakhbara	to enquire
'unf	violence
mujrim	criminal
ihtiyāt	precaution
qā'a	hall
imtana'a 'an	to refrain from
dharrī	atomic
taraddada ilā	to frequent
shibh (pl. ashbāh, shabah)	similarity
sila	connection
wadda	to wish, like
arshada	to guide, teach
qasada	to intend
istaghalla	to utilise, exploit
wijha nadar	viewpoint
(pl. wijhāt nadar)	
ba'uda 'an	to be distant from
manaha	to grant

Unit 75

qabīla (*pl.* qabā'il)	tribe
kāfaha	to struggle against
mustawsaf	clinic
intaqala	to be transferred
mudāhara	demonstration
istashāra	to consult
muhtamal	probable
jism (*pl.* ajsām)	body
al-'Irāq	Iraq
i'tiyādi	usual
shubbāk (*pl.* shabābik)	window
ghāba ('an)	to be absent (from)
jarīma (*pl.* jarā'im)	crime
qawwā	to strengthen
jarīh (*pl.* jarhā)	wounded
haraba	to flee
tāwula	table
qunsul (*pl.* qanāsil)	consul
alahha 'alā	to press
ta'ammala fī	to consider

Unit 76

daríba (*pl.* darā'ib)	tax
'a'ada	to prepare, make ready
nidāfa	cleanliness
isti'mār	imperialism
taklíf (*pl.* takālíf)	cost, expenses
al-mughfūr lahu	the late ...
bu'd	distance
basharíyya	mankind
iftakhara bi	to be proud of
mashrū' (*pl.* mashārí')	plan
jāhil (*pl.* juhhāl)	ignorant
wasíla (*pl.* wasā'il)	means
mu'allif	author, composer
musakkar	closed
akmala	to complete
ta'arrada	to oppose
ilzāmí	compulsory
sā'ada 'alā	to help
mínā' (*pl.* mawāni)	port
ihtarama	to honour

Unit 77

malīyya	finance
qadr (*pl.* aqdār)	amount
umrān	civilisation
manfa'a (*pl.* manāfi')	benefit
masdar (*pl.* masādir)	origin
muntasaf	middle
tajannaba	to avoid
nasīha (*pl.* nasā'ih)	advice
bakā	to cry
mustashār	adviser
shā'ir (*pl.* shu'arā)	poet
ra'asa	to preside over, lead
libās (*pl.* albisa)	clothing
Lubnān	Lebanon
wada'a	to put, lay
sayd	hunting
intadama	to be arranged
kharīf	autumn
khassasa	to specify
hammāl	porter

Unit 78

tilifūn	telephone
ikhtiyārī	optional
iltadhdha bi	to enjoy
hāsim	decisive
ittifāqan	by chance
mufrad	single
hādara	to lecture
majnūn (*pl.* majānīn)	mad
dhakar (*pl.* dhukūr)	male
safā	to be clear
'ibāra	phrase
mu'addal	average
jā'iza (*pl.* jawā'iz)	prize
'azīma (*pl.* 'azā'im)	invitation
yabisa	to harden
ghinā'	singing
tamayyaza	to be distinguished
al-Urdun	Jordan
tabāhatha ma'a ... fī	to discuss ... with
sūf (*pl.* aswāf)	wool

Unit 79

tahaddatha	to talk
'adīm	lacking
rīf (*pl.* aryāf)	country(side)
naddama	to organise
mashā'ir	feelings
ashrafa 'alā	to be about to
lahhām	butcher
jinsīyya	nationality
sīnamā	cinema
istadama bi	to collide with
ummī	illiterate
maq'ad (*pl.* maqā'id)	seat
tahālafa	to become allied with
hallāq	hairdresser
a'raj (*pl.* 'arj)	lame
ta'allaqa (bi)	to be fastened (to) (with)
ujra (*pl.* ujūr)	hire
'amma	paternal aunt
dalama	to oppress
hīla (*pl.* hiyal)	trick

Unit 80

tilifīsīyūn	television
shatt (*pl.* shutūt)	coast, shore
nahda	renaissance
tasāwā	to be equal with each other
nāqis	imperfect
inqilāb	revolution
khasama	to quarrel with
ahāta bi	to surround, acquaint with (ahāta 'ilman bi, to inform ... of)
'addala	to amend, revise
kayfīyya	condition
iltazama	to be obliged (to)
shi'r (*pl.* ash' ār)	poem, poetry
rukn (*pl.* arkān)	corner
'aqd (*pl.* 'uqūd)	contract
wahshī	wild
ashkala	to be different
uslūb (*pl.* asālīb)	method, way
hafida	to protect, learn by heart
sa'ida	to climb
tadhakkara	to remember

Unit 81

sāha	court(yard)
rādīyū	radio
hakā	to tell
shuhra	fame
sāda	to reign, rule
masīr (*pl.* masā'ir)	fate, future
nādiran	seldom
intafa'a (bi)	to take advantage (of)
samīm	genuine, true
dhakā'	intelligence
nahada	to rise
ightasala	to wash (oneself)
jādd	serious
qanāt (*pl.* qanawāt)	canal
taqā'ada	to retire
tuhma (*pl.* tuham, tuhmāt)	accusation
murāsil	correspondence
midfa' (*pl.* madāfi')	gun
dakhkhana	to smoke
fashila	to fail

Unit 82

nufūdh	influence
mas'ūlīyya	responsibility
saqata	to fall, fail
tibb	medicine
izdāda	to increase (*intrans.*)
khālid	immortal
tadammana	to include
akīd	certain
bādala ... bi	to exchange ... for
'amdān	intentionally
haddada (bi)	to threaten (with)
ijmā'ī	unanimous
musta'mara	colony
khatīr	serious
hakīm (*pl.* hukamā')	wise man, doctor
tas-hīlāt	facilities
tajawwala	to tour
hassās	sensitive
khayyāt	tailor
intalaqa	to depart

Unit 83

dafa'a	to pay, push
farraqa	to separate
batî'	slow
istashmara	to exploit, invest
'adāla	justice
aqlaqa	to disturb
jaddada	to renew
mubashāratan	immediately
ittakhadha	to take
sha'r	hair
lāhada	to notice
bātil	useless
tabaqa	category
wazza'a ('alā)	to distribute (to)
hikāya	story
khalîj (*pl.* khuljān)	gulf
ramā (bi)	to throw (ramā ilā, to aim at)
filāha	agriculture
silk (*pl.* aslāk)	wire (lā silkî, wireless)
nāfasa	to compete with

Unit 84

taqrîr (*pl.* taqārîr)	report
qalaba	to (over)turn
'ajūz (*pl.* 'ajā'iz)	old person
tadakhkhala	to interfere
mahhada	to prepare
niyāba	substitution
akhtā'	to be mistaken
qāmūs (*pl.* qawāmîs)	dictionary
sahhala	to facilitate
tālamā	for a long time
istaqalla	to be independent
sawāb	correct judgment
ihtafada (bi)	to save, preserve
masaha	to survey
farāgh	emptiness, leisure
dalla	to last
sulūk	behaviour
ghalā fî	to exaggerate
farāqa	to part from
za'îm (*pl.* zu'amā')	leader/brigadier

Unit 85

jasīm (*pl.* jisām)	vast, huge
hilf (*pl.* ahlāf)	treaty
ittahada	to unite (*intrans.*)
khirrīj	graduate
ajjala	to postpone
munkhafid	low (lying)
tatallaba	to demand, need
unshā (*pl.* ināsh)	female
i'tarada 'alā	to object to
mu'aqqad	complex
farra	to escape
sudfatan	by chance
qallada	to imitate
faj'atan	suddenly
nabā' (*pl.* anbā')	information, news
za'ila	to be angry
di'f	double
tālaba	to claim
naqasa	to decrease
harfīyyan	literally

Unit 86

silsila (*pl.* salāsil)	chain
nādala	to struggle with
turāb	earth
mutahaddith	spokesperson
khayma (*pl.* khaym, khiyām)	tent
manshā' (*pl.* manāshā')	source
gharad (*pl.* aghrād)	purpose
thāra	to rebel
ratb (*pl.* ritāb)	wet
'amūdi	vertical
mulāhada	observation
muqtadir	able
masrah (*pl.* masārih)	theatre
bākhira (*pl.* bawākhir)	steamship
tabbaqa	to apply
hārat	quarter, district
dayr (*pl.* adīra)	monastery
rayb	doubt
zabūn (*pl.* zabā'in)	customer
khazīna (*pl.* khazā'in)	treasury

Unit 87

mudhakkar	masculine
mu'āhida	treaty
bāraka	to bless
nātiq	spokesperson
mu'āwin	assistant
ladhīdh (*pl.* lidhādh)	delicious
shab'an	satisfied
inqasama (ilā)	to be divided (into)
armala (*pl.* arāmil)	widow
hasād	harvest
masqat ra'si	birthplace
taharraka	to move (*intrans.*)
iqlīm (*pl.* aqālīm)	region
sawwata	to vote
kaffa 'an	to desist from
miy'ād (*pl.* mawā'id)	rendezvous
abāha li	to permit to
qāhil	dry, barren
tabayyana	to appear, realise
kawwama	to heap

Unit 88

dhū	owner of, having the characteristic of
mutlaqan, 'alā 'l-itlāq	absolutely
kawwana	to create
masāfa	distance
wazana	to weigh (*trans.*)
sulta	authority
tamthīlī	representative, dramatic
raqqā	to promote
sākhin, sukhn	hot
muhām	lawyer
kafā'a	efficiency
salbī	negative
qisma	fate
rafī'	thin, high
aflaha	to succeed
muqāta'a	province
sadr (*pl.* sudūr)	breast, chest
ahmaq (*pl.* humq, hamqa)	stupid
dhanb (*pl.* dhunūb)	sin, guilt
hatman	inevitable

Unit 89

harāra	heat, temperature
qallamā	seldom
istakhdama	to use, employ
sahāfî	journalist
tadākhala	to intervene
nashāt	activity
marrana	to exercise
wassakha	to make dirty
ihtamma (bi)	to take an interest (in)
mustawda'	store
jidd	diligent
ayyada	to support
qitāl	battle
mu'annath	feminine
khātaba	to address
khasîb, khasib	fertile
rabî'	spring
qamh	wheat
akhras (*pl.* khurs)	dumb
hayawî	vital

Unit 90

atā	to come (atā bi, to bring)
khatt (*pl.* khutūt)	line, writing
ghalaba	to defeat
khāla	maternal aunt
nawā	to intend
rukhsa (*pl.* rukhas)	permit, licence
wadda'a	to say goodbye to
khasm (*pl.* khusūm)	opponent
izā'	opposite to
hujja (*pl.* hujaj)	plea, proof
ajma'a ('alā)	to agree (on)
sijn (*pl.* sujūn)	jail
muqaddima	preface
asarra ('alā)	to insist (on)
hayy'a	organisation
istayqata	to awake
sawād	blackness
inqalaba	to be overthrown
kammala	to complete
qadā	to judge, carry out (qadā 'alā, to sentence)

Unit 91

mubakkir	early
'umūq (*pl.* a'māq)	depth
tadrīban	gradually
iqtidā	to demand
athāth	furniture
awja'a	to hurt
dīmūqrātīyya	democracy
ayqata	to awaken
taghallaba 'alā	to overcome
ghabī (*pl.* aghbiyā')	stupid
ankara	to deny
ashbaha	to resemble
dayn (*pl.* duyūn)	debt
khalīfa (*pl.* khulafā')	caliph
ishtakā 'ilā (min)	to complain to (of)
hadaf (*pl.* ahdāf)	goal
mufawwadīyya	legation
imtiyāz	concession
kanīsa (*pl.* kanā'is)	church
hiyād	neutrality

Unit 92

musība (*pl.* masā'ib)	misfortune, bad luck
tarada	to send away
shabīh bi	similar to
āmana bi	to believe in
saraqa	to steal
'unsur (*pl.* 'anāsir)	element
khutba (*pl.* khutab)	speech
istabdala	to exchange
nafar (*pl.* anfār)	individual
istafsara	to enquire
mawwana	to supply
shuyū'īyya	communism
idtarra (ilā)	to force, compel (to)
aqallīyya	minority
tasālaha	to become reconciled
khulq (*pl.* akhlāq)	character (*pl.* morals)
istahāla	to change (*intrans.*), to be impossible
fidda	silver
istad'a	to summon
shāraka ... fī	to share with ... in

Unit 93

majjānî	free (*adj.*)
jarraba	to test
alghā	to cancel
dhakkara	to remind
sharaf	honour
tahammala	to bear
istaghna 'an	to dispense with
mîzānîyya	budget
malā'	to fill
mukhlis	loyal
firqa (*pl.* firaq)	team, group
ihtajja ('alā)	to plead, protest (against)
istāda	to hunt
ma'lūf	common
nadā	to call
jadwal	schedule, list, agenda
unbūb (*pl.* anābîb)	pipe
daw' (*pl.* adwā')	light
bisāt (*pl.* busut)	carpet
adarra bi	to harm

Unit 94

ad-dunyā	the world
daraj (*pl.* adrāj)	stairs
sallā	to pray
mawz	bananas
afragha	to empty
tamannā	to wish
tumaththil	representative, actor
harf (*pl.* hurūf)	letter (of alphabet)
muhāsib	accountant
ashghala	to occupy
darā	to know
athāra	to arouse
kallafa ... bi	to charge
farada	to suppose
tawaqqafa	to stop (*intrans.*) tawaqqafa 'alā (to depend on)
sayf (*pl.* suyūf)	sword
ab'ada	to exile
ta'ajjaba min	to marvel at
hākama	to prosecute
ahsā	to calculate

Unit 95

shujā' (*pl.* shuj'ān)	brave
ufqi	horizontal
harrama	to forbid
malān bi	full of
istaqarra	to settle
mā'iz (*pl.* mawā'iz)	goat (*collectively,* ma'z, goats)
'attala	to delay
qitā'	zone
'ashīra (*pl.* 'ashā'ir)	tribe
naqqaba ('an)	to explore (for)
'izz	glory
walada	to give birth to
ta'ahhada bi	to contract to
sama' (*pl.* samāwāt)	sky
dimāgh (*pl.* admigha)	brain
istahdafa	to aim (at)
'udwan	hostility
khālis	clear
qawiya	to become strong
habb (*pl.* hubūb)	seeds

Unit 96

mukhtir	dangerous
sarāha	clarity, candour
ra's māl	capital
(*pl.* ru'ūs amwāl)	
aqrada	to lend
khabbāz	baker
ghāmiq	dark-coloured
wāfir	abundant
mutlaq	unlimited
ishtāqa ilā	to long for
hamāqa	stupidity
arrakha	to set a date to
i'tamada 'alā	to rely on
harām	forbidden, prohibited
maqarr	headquarters
ihtawā	to include
istawlā 'alā	to take possession of
majjānan	free (*adv.*)
tamassa'a	to widen (*intrans.*)
istalaha	to be reconciled
infajara	to explode (*intrans.*)

Unit 97

sīgha (*pl.* siyagh)	form
iltizām (*pl.* iltizāmāt)	obligation, concession
kāffatan	all
baththa	to spread
'amūd (*pl.* a'mida)	column
sawiya	to be worth
imtadda (ilā)	to extend (to)
'abathan	in vain
dawrīyya	patrol
sā'ir	remainder
iqtaraha 'alā	to suggest
jadalan	for the sake of argument
masāha	survey (*n.*)
ista'adda	to be prepared
buhayra	lake
ufq (*pl.* āfāq)	horizon
kūra (*pl.* kurāt)	ball
shikāya	complaint
sabaha	to swim
imtāza ('alā) ... (bi)	to be distinguished (from)... (by)

Unit 98

wāha	oasis
'asīr	difficult
jazīl (*pl.* jizāl)	plentiful
haraqa	to burn
jābaha	to face
ittahama (bi)	to accuse ... (of)
timthāl (*pl.* tamāthil)	statue
ta'akhkhara	to be late
darara (*pl.* adrār)	injury
samīn (*pl.* simān)	fat (*adj.*)
qaddara	to estimate, value
i'talāfī	allied, coalition (*adj.*)
khutta (*pl.* khutat)	plan, diagram
mu'assasa	establishment
wajīh (*pl.* wujahā')	dignitary
iqtarada	to borrow
takrāran	repeatedly
qāta'a	to boycott
ishā'a	rumour
sādaqa 'alā	to confirm

Unit 99

awshaka 'alā	to be about to
mūsīqā	music
alamma bi	to become acquainted with
qārra	continent
intashara	to be spread
'asīr	juice
halaqa	to shave
nazla	cold (*n.*)
fasīh (*pl.* fusahā')	eloquent
yanbū' (*pl.* yanābi')	source
khutūra	seriousness
qimma (*pl.* qimam)	summit
istinā'i	artificial
mayyaza	to distinguish
qafaza	to jump
badr (*pl.* budūr)	full moon
gharasa	to plant
saqf (*pl.* suqūf)	ceiling
salaba	to rob
qunsulīyya	consulate

Unit 100

sinn (*pl.* asnān)	tooth
barrad	refrigerator
hamām, hamāma	pigeon
massāh	surveyor
tawazza'a	to be distributed
qamīs (*pl.* qumsān)	shirt
fasāha	eloquence
jabbār (*pl.* jabāra)	giant
tamyīz	discrimination
qabīh (*pl.* qibāh)	ugly
shakwa	complaint
hilāl (*pl.* ahilla)	crescent moon
udhn (*pl.* ādhān)	ear
sanad	document, deed
marāfiq	amenities
inbathaqa min	to arise from, derive from
sayyād	hunter
tatawwa'a	to volunteer
saddaqa	to believe
kawma (*pl.* akwām)	heap

Arabic Index

Because the index is intended for anglophone readers, the index is arranged by the letters of the Arabic alphabet in *English word order,* so that 'ain and hamza are ignored.

'amala 14
'amalī 45
'amalīyya 51
amāma 34
amāna 59
āmana bi 92
amara 32
amdā 51
'amdān 82
'āmil 56, 71
'amila 8
amīn 24
amina 27
'amīq 33
amīr 38
amkana 6
'āmm 14
'amm 66
'amma 79
ammā...aw 44
ammā ... fa 7
'ammara 49
amn 39
amr 20
Amrīkā 63
ams 3
'amūd 97
'amūdī 86
an 1
'an 3
anā 1
'anā 29
anfaqa 49
anhā 60
'anīf 36
anīs 64
ānisa 65
ankara 91
anna 2
anshā' 26
anta 2
antaja 20
anti 3
antum 3
antunna 7
'aqaba 51
aqada 33

aqallīyya 92
aqāma 26
'aqd 80
'aqiba 62
'āqiba 51
'āqil 11
'aql 15
aqlaqa 83
aqrada 96
'arab 2
arāda 11
aradā 73
'arada 19
'ārada 40
'arafa 9
a'raj 79
ard 17
'arīd 42
'arīda 69
arjah 64
armala 87
'arrafa 52, 1
arrakha 96
arsala 11
arshada 74
aruzz 18
asāba 65
asarra 'alā 90
asās 40
asbaha 13
asdara 63
asfar 35
ashā' 30
'ashā' 24
āsha 45
ashāra 43, 60
ashbaha 91
ashghala 94
ashīra 95
ashkala 80
ashrafa 'alā 79
āsif 44
'āsima 28
'asīr 98, 99
Āsiyā 65
'askarī 21
asl 34

aslaha 34
aslī 27
asmā 12
asmar 32
'asr 43
asra'a 38
'asrī 29
assasa 38
aswad 11
'atā 12
atā 90
atā'a 61
atāha li 26
atamma 34
athara 39
athāra 94
'athara 'alā 56
athāth 91
aththara 27
'atīq 63
'atisha 68
atrash 69
'attala 95
aw 1
'awā'id 26
awdaha 54
awja'a 91
awjada 51
'awn 71
awqafa 32
awshaka 'alā 99
awwal 4
aydan 3
'ayn 10
ayna 4
ayqata 91
ayyada 89
'ayyana 43
ayyī 22
ayyi? 7
'azama 70
'azīma 78
'azīz 25
azma 37
azraq 10

102

bāʾa 26
baʾatha 51
bāb 9
baʾd 1, 4
badā 25
badaʾa 24
baʾdaʾdhin 56
bādala ... bi 82
badan 73
badawī 25
baddala 57
badhala 41
bādiya 30
badr 99
baghtatan 48
bahatha 17
bāhatha .. fī 27
bahr 8
baʾīd 9
bāʾith 59
bakā 77
bākhira 86
bākir 62
bal 13
balad 7
baladīyya 39
balāgh 24
balagha 31
bālagha fī 72
balīgh 73
banā 20
bank 19
bannaʾ 69
banzīn 46
baqara 32
baqī 69
baqīyya 62
baqqāl 68
baraka 60
bāraka 87
baraza 64
barīd 19
bārid 14
bārih, al- 6
bāriha, al- 6
barlamān 29
barnāmaj 48

barr 70
barrād 100
barrara 71
bas 2
basata 53
bashar 63
bāshara bi 64
basharī 70
basharīyya 76
basīt 25
baʾtha 58
baththa 97
batīʾ 83
bātil 83
baʾuda ʾan 74
bayān 19
bayd 18
bayna 3
baynamā 14
bayt 3
bayyana 62
bi 1
bidʾ 24
bidaʾa 63
biʾīr 66
bijānibi 34
bikhusūs 7
bilād 10
bilqurbi min 21
bin 5
bināʾ 57
bināya 46
bint 8
biʾr 59
birka 13
bisabab 5
bisāt 93
bisurʾa 47
biwāsita 73
buʾd 76
buhayra 97
bukhār 62
bukra 3
bulīs 12
bustān 27

daʾā 11
daʾā ilā 20
dabbara 58
dābit 37
dafaʾa 83
dāfaʾa 31
dahara 18
dahika 41
dahisha 49
dahr 49
daʾīf 17
dāʾiman 3
dāʾira 40
dakhala 18
dākhil 4
dākhilī 26
dakhkhana 81
dakhl 65
dakhm 51
dalāla 48
dalām 63
dalama 79
dalīl 65
dalla 84
dalla ʾalā 35
dam 57
dāma 45
damina 57
danna 16
daqīq 29
daqīqa 16
darā 94
dāra 61
daraba 14
daraj 94
daraja 29
darara 98
darasa 17
darb 62
darf 28
darība 76
darrasa 32
dars 27
darūra 27
darūrī 23
dawʾ 93
daʾwa 42, 59

dawla 34
dawra 64
dawrīyya 97
dayf 38
dayn 91
dayr 86
dayyiq 25
dh. *See after* duwalī
di'aya 27
didda 72
di'f 85
difā' 38
dill 56
dimāgh 95
dīmūqrātīyya 91
dīmūqrātīyyu 63
dīn 45
dīnār 52
dirāsa 15
dirham 47
dīwān 50
diyāfa 66
duhr, ad- 20
dukkān 17
dūlār 71
dūna 24
dunyā, ad- 94
dustūr 57
duwalī 6

dhahab 44
dhahaba 6
dhakā' 81
dhakar 78
dhakara 12
dhakī 34
dhakkara 93
dhālika 1
dhanb 88
dharrī 74
dhatī 53
dhātu 44
dhū 88

fa 1
fa'ala 9
faddala 46
fadī' 64
fadīla 71
fadl 56
fadlan 'an 52
fahasa 52
fahima 21
fā'ida 17
fā'iq 63
fāja' 70
faj'atan 85
fajr 71
fākhir 63
fākiha 32
fakka 55
fakkara fī 26
fallāh 18
falsafa 55
fann 54
fannī 38
faqat 2, 4
faqīr 66
far' 50
farada 94
farāgh 84
farah 54
farāqa 84
faras 24
fard 47
farhān 41
farīd 71
fārigh 66
farih 68
farīq 34
farq 50
farra 85
farraqa 83
fasāha 100
fashila 81
fasīh 99
fasl 36
fassala 58
fassara 72
fata 43
fataha 7

fatāt 55
fātih 37
fattasha 39
fatūr 32
fāwada 57
fawqa 2
fī 1
fidda 92
fikra 30
filāha 83
film 69
finjān 18
firāsh 24
firqa 93
fitr 32
fulān 68
fulūs 7
funduq 29
fursa 38

ghāba min 75
ghabī 91
ghadā' 25
ghadan 3
ghādara 52
ghadbān 58
ghadiba 'alā 29
ghā'ib 39
ghalā fī 84
ghalaba 90
ghalat 49
ghāli 7
ghāliban 53
ghalita 52
ghalta 49
ghāmiq 96
ghanam 17
ghanī 13
ghanna 42
gharad 86
gharasa 99
gharb 18
gharīb 31
ghasala 72
ghayr (anna) 18

ghayyara 45
ghinā' 78
ghurfa 31

habb 95
hadaf 91
hadāra 69
hadara 16
hādara 78
hadatha 16
hādatha 29
hadd 19
hādd 67
haddād 51
haddada 38
haddada bi 82
haddara 42
hādha 1
hādhihi 1
hādhir 6
hadīd 46
hadīqa 10
hadīth 18, 39
hādith 22
hadīya 48
hafada 'alā 36
haffada 64
hafida 80
hafla 12
hā'it 21
hāja 30
hajama 'alā 66
hājama 70
hakā 81
hakadhā 15
hakama 30
hākama 94
hakīm 82
hākim 36
hal 2
hāl 5
hāla 22, 73
hālaman 50
hālan 32
halaqa 99

hālī 35
halīb 60
halīf 69
halla 21
hallāq 79
hamā 37
hamala 31
hamām 100
hamāqa 96
hamdu 2
hamla 37
hāmm 25
hammāl 77
handasa 26
hanī' 48
haqīqa 22
haqīqatan 54
haqq 17
haqqan 52
haqqaqa 21
haraba 75
hāraba 74
haraka 19
harām 96
haraqa 98
harāra 89
harasa 43
hārat 86
harb 38
harf 94
harfīyyan 85
hāris 50
harr 6
harrama 95
harrara 27
hasaba 28
hasād 87
hasala 15
hasan 12
hasbamā 61
hasiba 36
hāsim 78
hassana 37
hassās 82
hatab 51
hatman 88
hatta 21

hattā 6
hawā' 30
hāwala 20
hawālī 13
hawla 28
hawwala 63
haya 39
hayāt 59
hayawān 14
hayawī 89
haythu 33
hayy 11
hayy'a 90
hāza 10
hazīma 73
hazīn 58
hikāya 83
hikma 66
hīla 79
hilāl 100
hilf 85
himār 63
himma 58
hīn 21
hīna 14
hīna 'dhin 55
hinta 69
hisāb 39
hisān 36
hīya 1
hiyād 91
hizb 22
hubb 6
hujja 90
hukm 35
hukūma 3
hulw 25
hum 3
hunā 2
hunāka 2
hurr 40
hurrīyya 59
husn 28
hutayl 7
hūwa 1

105

kanîsa 91
karam 55
karama 56
karîm 9
karrama 61
ka's 22
kasaba 49
kasara 42
kashafa 55
kaslān 62
kataba 7
kātaba 9
kathîr 4
kātib 66
kawma 100
kawwama 87
kawwana 88
kay 21
kayf 2
kayfiyya 80
kh. *See after* kursî
kîlū 47
kîlūmitr 48
kitāb 10
kull 3
kullīyya 45
kūra 97
kursî 45

khabar 15
khabbāz 96
khabir 34
khada'a 72
khadama 37
khādim 16
khāfa 36
khafîf 27
khafîr 52
khāl 67
khāla 90
khālafa 66
khalaqa 72
khālid 82
khalîfa 91
khalîj 83

khālis 95
khallā 44
kharaja 13
kharîf 77
khārij 6
khārijî 23
khārita, kharîta 70
kharraba 46
kharūf 62
khās 3
khasama 80
khashab 64
khashin 67
khashiya 64
khasib, khasîb 89
khasira 60
khasm 90
khassa 40
khāssa 6
khassasa 77
khātaba 89
khatama 50
khatar 20
khatir 58
khatîr 82
khatt 90
khawwala 72
khayl 35
khayma 86
khayr 7, 20
khayyāt 82
khazana 42
khazîna 86
khazzān 51
khibra 36
khidma 12
khilāfan li 61
khilāl 31
khirrîj 85
khitām 56
khizāna 69
khubz 16
khulq 92
khusūsan 6
khusūsi 18
khutba 92
khutta 98

khutūra 99
khutwa 58

lā 1
labisa 15
ladā 25
ladhîdh 87
lāhada 83
lahda 28
lahhām 79
lahm 22
la'iba 44
lajna 72
lākin 4
lam 15
lammā 6
lan 20
laqiya 62
law 11
lawn 26
layla 4
laysa 14
latîf 15
lazima 37
li 1
li'anna 5
libās 77
lidhālika 14
likay 21
limā, limādhā 29
lisān 27
liss 51
Lubnān 77
lugha 19

mā 2, 4
mā' 4
mā lā ... abadan 38
mā zāla 14
ma'a 2
ma'an 53
ma'āsh 44
mabda' 49

mablagh 32
madā 53
madanī 26
madanīyya 46
madda 17
mādda 37
mādī 37
madīna 4
madkhal 39
madrasa 22
maftūh 22
Maghrib 66
mahabba 38
mahall 25
mahallī 46
mahara fī 72
mahatta 12
mahdūd 45
mahhada 84
ma'hid 54
mahkama 37
mahsūl 62
mā'ida 32
ma'īsha 49
mā'iz 95
majāl 62
majalla 42
majhūl 65
majjānan 96
majjānī 93
majmū' 41
majnūn 78
majran 60
makān 29
makhfar 51
makhraj 35
makhzan 54
makkana 71
maktaba 39
maktal 31
maktūb 63
māl 46
malā' 93
malaka 7
malān bi 95
malik 4
malika 34

malīyya 77
ma'lūf 93
ma'mal 45
mamlaka 23
mamnū'a 6
man 5
ma'nā 47
mana'a 24
manaha 74
ma'nawī 58
mandar 54
mandūb 36
manfa'a 77
manshā' 86
manzil 40
maq'ad 79
maqāl 42
maqarr 96
maqsid 62
ma'qūl 20
mar' 35
mar'a, al- 16
marad 22
marāfiq 100
marhala 58
ma'rid 61
marīd 16
ma'rifa 24
markab 28
markaz 11
marra 11
marrana 89
marsūm 53
martaba 53
masa' 7
mas'ā 42
masāfa 88
masaha 84
masāha 97
masaka 44
mas'ala 56
masdir 77
mashā 4
mashā'ir 79
mashghūl 40
mashhūr 27
mashriq 23

mashrū' 76
mashrūb 67
masīhī 49
masīr 81
masjid 42
maskan 20
maslaha 21
masna' 39
masqat 87
masrah 86
masrif 42
masrūf 40
massāh 100
mas'ūl 34
mas'ūlīyya 82
matā 4
māta 17
mata'm 16
matar 30
matār 47
matara 33
matba'a 62
matbakh 38
matbū'āt 54
mathaf 47
mathalan 20
mathl 31
maththala 37
matlab 56
mawadda 73
mawdi' 36
mawdū' 14
maw'id 61
mawqi' 46
mawqif 16
mawrid 55
mawsim 32
mawwala 70
mawwana 92
mawt 12
mawz 94
maydān 48
mayyaza 99
mayyit 17
mazra'a 28
midfa' 81
miftāh 62

109

milh 15
min 1
mīnā' 76
mintaqa 19
miskīn 58
Misr 19
mithāl 22
mithāq 68
mithl 14
mitr 45
miy'ād 87
mīzānīyya 93
mu'addal 78
mu'āhida 87
mu'akhkhiran 59
mu'allif 76
mu'allim 26
mu'annath 89
mu'aqqad 85
mu'aqqat 65
mu'āsir 29
mu'askar 67
mu'assasa 98
mu'āwin 87
mubakkir 91
mubashāratan 83
mubāshir 65
mudāhara 75
mu'dam 61
mudawwar 70
mudda 31
mudhakkar 87
mudhik 41
mudīr 21
mudlim 68
mufattish 59
mufawwadīyya 91
mufīd 14
mufrad 78
mughfūr lahu 76
muhādara 51
muhālafa 41
muhām 88
muhandis 24
muharrir 59
muhāsib 94
muhimm 18

muhīt 64
muhtamal 75
mujrim 74
mujtahid 33
mujtama'a 64
muka"ab 73
mukhlis 93
mukhtir 96
mulāhada 86
mumkin 4
mumtāz 45
munaddama 65
munāsaba 49
mundhu 7
munkhafid 85
muntasaf 77
muqaddima 90
muqāta'a
muqbil 59
muqtadir 86
murabba' 63
murajjah 73
murāqib 74
murāsil 81
murīh 50
murr 36
musakkar 76
mushkila 15
musība 92
mūsīqā 99
Muslim 5
mustadīr 64
musta'mara 82
mustaqbil 40
mustaqīm 57
mustashār 77
mustashfā 43
mustawda' 89
mustawī 49
mustawsaf 75
mu'tadil 60
mutahaddith 86
mutakallim 70
mu'tamar 67
mutawāsil 71
mutlaq 96
mutlaqan 88

muwaddif 15
muwaqqat 65
muwātin 52
muzāri' 56

nāba 31
nabā 85
nabbaha ilā 47
nadā 93
nādala 86
nadara ilā 10
nadaran li 52
nadarī 46
nadarīyya 56
naddafa 67
naddama 79
nādi 44
nadīf 33
nādiran 81
nafā 70
nafaqa 50
nafar 92
nāfasa 83
naffadha 30
nafi'a 68
nafiqa 56
nafs 3
naft 21
nahada 81
nahār 17
nahda 80
nāhiya 65
nahnu 7
nahr 21
nahw 60
nahwa 38
nā'ib 22
nā'im 59
najaha 61
nakhl 33
nāla 45
na'm 2
nāma 46
naqala 36
nāqasha 43

naqd 61
nāqis 80
naqqaba 95
nār 32
nāsaba 50
nasaha 48
nashā' 35
nashara 34
nashāt 89
nashifa 70
nashīt 36
nashra 36
nasīha 77
nasiya 44
nataja 13
natīja 20
nātiq 87
naw' 20
nawā 90
nawawī 64
nazala 17
nazla 99
nidāfa 76
nidām 30
nihāya 48
nisba 41
nisf 38
nitāq 69
niyāba 84
nufūdh 82
nuqta 49
nūr 45
nuskha 46

qā'a 74
qa'ada 68
qabada 45
qābala 22
qabīh 100
qabila 12
qabīla 75
qabla 2
qabr 44
qad 5
qadā 90

qadam 24
qadara 15
qaddama 66
qaddara 98
qādi 57
qadīm 8
qādim 32
qadima 10
qadīyya 68
qadr 77
qafaza 99
qāhil 87
qahwa 8
qā'id 31
qā'ida 58
qā'ima 31
qāla 4
qal'a 60
qalaba 84
qalam 12
qalb 32
qalīl 9
qallada 85
qallamā 89
qāma 6
qamar 23
qamh 89
qamīs 100
qāmūs 84
qanāt 81
qānūn 11
qara'a 20
qārana bi 55
qarār 43
qarīb 10
qarīban 45
qarn 49
qārra 99
qarrara 38
qarya 23
qasada 74
qasama 19
qasr 9
qata'a 25
qāta'a 98
qatala 17
qātala 26

qatīl 39
qāwama 72
qawī 10
qawiya 95
qawm 19
qawmī 28
qawwā 75
qīma 40
qimma 99
qism 11
qisma 88
qissa 19
qit'a 33
qita' 95
qitāl 89
qitār 48
qiwām 71
qiyāda 67
qumāsh 66
qunsul 75
qunsulīyya 99
Qur'ān 8, 19
qutn 50
qutr 54
quwwa 17

ra'ā 38
ra'asa 77
rabata 53
rabī' 89
rabiha 44
rābita 57
radd 41
radda 40
radī' 25
radia 73
rādiyū 81
rafa'a 20
rafada 60
rāfaqa 56
rafī' 88
rafīq 41
raghba 60
raghiba 53
rāha 42

111

rahhaba 61
rā'iha 68
ra'īs 7
ra'īsī 16
rajā 63
raja'a 17
rajul 3
rakada 44
rakhīs 8
rākib 35
rakiba 36
ramā 83
raml 26
rāqaba 59
raqm 23
raqqā 88
ra's 47
ra's māl 96
rasama 48
rasm 53
rasmī 13
rasūl 16
ratb 86
rātib 46
rattaba 48
ra'y 26
rayb 86
rīf 79
rīh 43
rihla 45
rijl 22
risāla 23
riyāl 32
rubba 61
rubbamā 47
rūh 47
rukhsa 90
rukn 80
rutba 51
ruzz 18

sa'a 4
sa'ā 52
sā'ada 'alā
sa'ala 15

sa'b 14
sabab 16
sabāh 5
sabaha 97
sabaqa 19
sabbaba 66
sabī 24
sābiq 12
sābiqan 47
sāda 81
sadāqa 47
sādaqa 'alā 98
sadara 27
sadda 46
saddaqa 100
saddara 35
sadīq 9
sādiq 57
sādir 37
sadr 88
safā 78
safar 39
sāfara 24
safh 72
safha 62
safīna 37
safīr 71
saghīr 8
sāha 81
sāha bi 22
sāhaba 70
sahāfa 33
sahāfī 89
sahha 13
sahhala 84
sāhib 10
sahīfa 40
sahīh 10
sāhil 31
sahl 13
sahn 46
sahrā' 44
sa'īda 80
sā'ih 59
sā'in 43
sā'iq 57
sā'ir 97

sajīn 63
sajjāda 43
sajjāla 59
sakana 50
sākhin 88
sākin 38
salaba 99
salafan 61
salahīyya 71
salām 6
salāma 65
salbī 88
sālih 12
sālim 12
salīm 26
sallā 94
sallaha 36
sallama 21
sama' 95
samaha 19
samak 25
sami'a 19
samīm 81
sāmin 57
samīn 98
sana 9
sāna 30
sana'a 20
sanad 100
sanawī 32
sāqa 38
saqata 82
saqf 99
sāra 10
sarafa 24
sarāha 96
saraqa 92
sarī' 27
sarīh 72
sarra 68
sarrāf 65
sarraha 57
sath 34
sathī 50
sawā 69
sawāb 84
sawād 90

112

unshā 85
'unsur 92
'unsurī 68
'unwān 53
'uqūba 73
Urdun, al- 78
Urūba 32
usbu' 57
usbū' 41
'usfūr 69
uslūb 80
ustādh 16
'utla 53

wa 1
wa'ada 70
wad' 35
wada'a 77
wadda 74
wadda'a 90
wādi 64
wadīfa 71
wādih 31
wafāh 71
wāfaqa 'alā 34
wafd 24
waffaqa 22
wāfir 96
wāha 98
wāhad 1
wahda 21
wahhada 29
wahīd 58
wahshī 80
wajaba 'alā 12
wajada 12
wājaha 11
wajh 30
wājib 26
wājid 2

wajīh 98
wajjaha 67
wakīl 27
walad 5
walada 95
walākin 4
walāsīyyamā 28
wāli 26
walia 53
wālid 35
waqa'a 15
waqafa 39
wāqi'a 47
waqqa'a 52
waqt 7
waqt'idhin 55
wara'a 22
warada 49
waraq 12
waraqa 18
wāridāt 53
wasafa 51
wasākha 69
wasala 11
wāsala 54
wasat 19
wasf 60
wāsi' 34
wasi'a 13
wasikh 36
wasīla 76
wāsita 28
wassa'a 29
wassakha 89
watan 9
watanī 6
wathīq 43
wathiqa 31
wathīqa 57
wazana 88
wazīr 5

wazza'a 83
wifqan li 55
wijdān 48
wijha nadar 74
wikāla 34
wilāya 29
wizāra 3
wudūh 67

yabisa 78
yad 24
yadawī 32
yamīn 23
yanbaghī li 51
yanbu' 99
yasār 23
yawm 3

za'ama 55
zabūn 86
zāda 38
za'ila 85
za'īm 84
za'lān 71
zaman 9
zamīl 64
zāra 5
zara'a 21
zawaj 23
zawj 31
zawja 36
zawwada 66
zayt 28
zaytūn 67
zirā'a 40
zubda 35
zujāj 11

English Index

116

120

121

124

permission 30, 42, 55
permit 90
permit, to 19, 26, 57
permit to, to 87
person 4, 9, 18
personality 23
petition 69
petrol 46
philosophy 55
photograph, to 44
phrase 78
picture 23
piece 33
pigeon 100
pipe 93
place 25, 29, 36, 46
plan 70, 76, 98
plant, to 99
plantation 28
plate 46
play, to 44
plea 90
plead, to 93
pleasant 15, 48
please, to 68, 73
pleased with, to be 52
plentiful 98
poem 80
poet 77
poetry 80
poetry anthology 50
point 49
point to, to 35
police 12, 15
police post 51
polite to, to be 71
political 11
politician 11
politics 23
pool 13
poor 58, 66
port 76
porter 77
positive 68
possess, to 7, 8
possible 4
possible, to be 6

post (office) 19
postage stamp 56
postpone, to 85
pound 51
power 55
practical 45
praise 2
pray, to 11, 94
precaution 74
precede, to 19, 59
preface 90
prefer, to 46
prepare, to 76, 84
prepared, to be 97
present 6, 35
present at, to be 16, 58
preserve, to 84
preside over, to 77
president 7
press 33, 66
press, printing 62
press, to 75
pretend, to 55
prevent, to 73
previous 12
previously 47
price 43, 63
Prince 38
principal 16
principle 49
print, to 42
printed matter 54
printing press 62
prisoner 63
prize 78
probable 64, 73, 75
problem 15, 56
proceed, to 53
produce, to 20
professor 16
profit, to 68
profits 26
programme 48
progress 59
prohibit, to 24
prohibited 6, 96
promise 26

promise, to 70
promote, to 88
proof 90
propaganda 27
property 46
prosecute, to 94
protect, to 30, 36, 37, 80
protest against, to 93
proud of, to be 76
proverb 31
province 29, 88
public 25, 31
publication 36
publish, to 34
punish, to 51
punishment 73
pupil 60
purpose 86
push, to 83
put, to 77
put down, to 21

qualification 71
quality 70
quantity 57
quarrel with, to 80
quarter 86
queen 34
question 33, 56, 68
question, to ask a 61
quick 27
quickly 47
quiet, to be 50

race 19
racial 68
radio 81
railway 55
rain 30
rain, to 33
raise, to 20
rank 51
reach, to 31, 42

125

OLEANDER LANGUAGE AND LITERATURE

LIBYA PAST AND PRESENT

APULEIUS ON TRIAL AT SABRATHA
Philip Ward

THE LIBYAN CIVIL CODE
I.M. Arif & M.O. Ansell

LIBYAN MAMMALS
Ernst Hufnagl

THE LIBYAN REVOLUTION
I.M. Arif & M.O. Ansell

MOTORING TO NALUT
Philip Ward

SABRATHA
Philip Ward

TRIPOLI
Philip Ward

BOOKS FROM OLEANDER

SPANISH KEY WORDS
Pedro Casal

ITALIAN KEY WORDS
Gianpaolo Intronati

FRENCH KEY WORDS
Xavier-Yves Escande

KING HUSAIN AND THE KINGDOM OF HEJAZ
Randall Baker

HA'IL: OASIS CITY OF SAUDI ARABIA
Philip Ward

REPORT ON A JOURNEY TO RIYADH (1865)
Lewis Pelly

THE GOLD-MINES OF MIDIAN
Sir Richard Burton

THE LAND OF MIDIAN
Sir Richard Burton

ARABIAN GULF INTELLIGENCE
comp. R.H. Thomas

TRIPOLI: PORTRAIT OF A CITY
Philip Ward

MONUMENTS OF SOUTH ARABIA
Brian Doe

ANNALS OF OMAN
Sirhan ibn Sirhan

MINISTER IN OMAN
Neil McLeod Innes

TRAVELS IN OMAN
Philip Ward

HISTORY OF SEYD SAID (1819) (Oman)
Vincenzo Maurizi

OMANI PROVERBS
A.S.G. Jayakar

ARABIA IN EARLY MAPS
G.R. Tibbetts

BAHRAIN: A TRAVEL GUIDE
Philip Ward